Haunted Maine Lighthouses

Taryn Plumb

Down East Books

Camden, Maine

Down East Books

An imprint of The Rowman & Littlefield Publishing Group, Inc.
4501 Forbes Blvd., Ste. 200
Lanham, MD 20706
www.rowman.com
Distributed by NATIONAL BOOK NETWORK

British Library Cataloguing in Publication Information available

Library of Congress Cataloging-in-Publication Data
Names: Plumb, Taryn, 1981– author.
Title: Haunted Maine lighthouses / Taryn Plumb.
Description: Camden, Maine : Down East Books, 2018. | Includes
   bibliographical references.
Identifiers: LCCN 2018016924 (print) | LCCN 2018020951 (ebook) | ISBN
   9781608939701 | ISBN 9781608939695 (pbk.)
Subjects: LCSH: Haunted lighthouses—Maine. | Lighthouses—Maine—Miscellanea.
Classification: LCC BF1476 (ebook) | LCC BF1476 .P58 2018 (print) | DDC
   133.109741—dc23
LC record available at https://lccn.loc.gov/2018016924

Sometimes, very often, you have to be your own beacon—
and that's when you realize you're the strongest one you have.

CONTENTS

Introduction

They are connected with elemental eloquences, fire and wind and ancient worshipping. They are houses almost as holy as churches, in the long history of man.

—Robert P. Tristram Coffin

Lighthouses are more than just guiding lights or picturesque beacons—they are standing metaphors, rife with symbolism.

First and foremost, we identify them with home and safety; they serve as an abiding welcome. But they are imbued with numerous other characteristics, as well: courage, determination, heroism; beauty, love, heartbreak; liberty, patriotism, democracy. They provide a perpetual warning and serve as a stand-in for God's devotional light (and wrath), and represent the enduring romanticism of the sea contrasted with its perilous dangers.

Not to mention the fact that they are simply stunning to behold, offering inspiration for countless artists and writers over the ages. And who, upon gazing at one of them, hasn't felt compelled to take a picture (or, more likely, several)?

Ultimately, lighthouses are intertwined with the history and mythos of the Pine Tree State. Maine simply wouldn't be Maine without them. They represent its rich maritime heritage and deep and profound natural beauty, and stand as significant landmarks of tourism.

And, of course, they wouldn't be complete without their ghosts.

These compelling structures come intricately interwoven with stories of the unknown, the unexplained, and the purely confounding.

Although Maine has been host to dozens of lighthouses, they ultimately haven't been able to fully prevent disaster; the waters off its coast are a literal graveyard of ships. The state's iconic beacons have stood as forlorn witnesses to numerous wrecks and drownings, have themselves withstood the vicious battering of the Atlantic, and have provided punishing settings for keepers and their families. Their pasts are also pockmarked by gruesome tales of cannibalism; ice-encrusted lovers; murder; suicide; and many an encounter with a lost or lingering soul.

Today, roughly sixty-five lighthouses (some still lit, others not) remain standing at their lookouts along the Maine shoreline.

The inquisitive mind can only imagine that each and every one of them harbors some sort of ghost—but while many do openly reveal themselves, others hold tight, never to divulge their mysteries and secrets.

Ceaseless Watch

Lighthouses are about as old as civilization itself: Ever since humans launched their first crudely built dory into the unknown waters of the sea, they have relied on sentinels to lead them back to safety.

The earliest guiding lights were said to be controlled fires set along rocky coastlines, or lanterns hung from moored boats. But it didn't take mariners long to realize that the higher up the light was set, the farther it could be seen, so the practice evolved to setting bonfires ablaze atop taller and taller precipices.

Fitting with the sheer grandeur of their respective dominions, the Greeks and Egyptians were said to be the first to erect stone beacons—many of which have long since tumbled into the sea—that served both as lighthouses and as magnificent entrance markers to ports.

Among those was the Colossus of Rhodes, built in 280 BCE as an homage to the Greek sun god Helios. Standing an imposing one hundred feet tall astride two pillars at the entrance of the Hellenic island's harbor, the enormous effigy held a torch that was lit by nightfall.

Meanwhile, one of the greatest shining sentinels known to humankind was the famed Lighthouse of Alexandria (also known as the Pharos of Alexandria) built by the Egyptian Ptolemaic kingdom between 280 and 247 BCE. Standing more than 325 feet, it held the distinction for centuries of being the tallest man-made structure in the world. It was said that it was constantly kept burning, its light seen for miles beyond the harbor of the long-destroyed city.

However, both ancient monuments were toppled by earthquakes—the Colossus in 224 BCE, the Alexandria lighthouse not until the thirteenth century—so they live on only in legend.

From the time of their existence, however, "Pharos" became a catch-all phrase for lighthouses, and the term "pharology" was eventually set down in permanent record in the mid-1800s to define the scientific study of lighthouses.

Not to be outdone, though, the Romans followed suit by building grandiose light towers all over their vastly expanding empire, and Europe took up the practice as it grew its influence and power.

But the Romans, as was their way, seem to have firmly maintained their dominance: The oldest-known standing lighthouse is the Tower of Hercules in western Spain, built by the empire in the first century. Square-shaped, topped with a glass dome and with a distinguishing stone finger jutting up to the sky, it stands roughly 180 feet tall on a stark peninsula overlooking the Coruna bay.

And as the old world began to set its influence upon the new one, settlers carried the lighthouse tradition across the seas with them.

As time went on and the colonies began to thrive, the structures were erected not just as a diversion to disaster, but to serve as a sort of "Open for Business" sign allowing coastal trade to prosper. The federal government took over their operation in 1789, with President George Washington himself taking a personal interest in them.

The first beacon in the American colonies was Boston Light, built in 1716 on Little Brewster Island in Boston Harbor. Its eighty-nine-foot tower still stands today, guarding one of the country's oldest continuously active ports.

Meanwhile, Maine's first lighthouse was Portland Head Light, completed in 1791 and serving as the quintessence of New England sentinels: a tall white stone tower accompanied by an idyllic-looking red-roofed house, standing atop a craggy jumble of rocks.

Ensuing lighthouses were built all along the state's watery borders, from York to Lubec (where the unique red-and-white candy-striped West Quoddy Head Light serves as the eastern-most point of the United States, welcoming the first spears of morning sun to hit the country), and they range in height from 20 to 130 feet.

Considered a feat of engineering, they were purposely created circularly shaped and tapered; that form was said to offer the best resistance to the pummeling ocean and elements. Meanwhile, their height was determined by how far out their designers intended for them to be seen, as well as the estimated force and height of the waves that used all of their brute force against them.

But as with anything, it was a process of trial and error, with many Maine lighthouses having to be rebuilt or refortified because the brutality of their environs was underestimated. For that same reason, many were also eventually equipped with fog signals or giant fog bells weighing thousands of pounds.

Initially, their lanterns were lit by open fire, then whale or vegetable oil—and then in the mid-1800s came the revolutionary Fresnel lens, a triumph of beauty and construction in and of itself. Developed by French physicist Augustin-Jean Fresnel, they consist of multiple layers of glass that are angled and cut to different lengths and thicknesses, ultimately giving off much more light than their predecessors—with the added bonus that they cost much less to keep lit. Proving their superior function, many still remain in use today.

Scottish lighthouse engineer Alan Stevenson (relative to renowned nineteenth-century author Robert Louis Stevenson), gushed of them: "Nothing can be more beautiful than an entire apparatus for a fixed light of the first order . . . I know no work of art more beautiful or creditable to the boldness, ardor, intelligence, and zeal of the artist."

Lighthouses served as active aids to navigation in Maine into the mid-1900s, even as keepers were slowly relieved over time, their jobs becoming defunct as lights were gradually automated. As air and rail became ever-preferred forms of transport, many lights were eventually decommissioned. Some (including subjects of this book) are still in use as active navigational aids under the US Coast Guard, while others are maintained by nonprofit organizations, educational institutions, or private entities. Many of Maine's lighthouses, whoever their caretakers, have also been given the distinction of being listed on the National Register of Historic Places.

Today, having made their lasting mark on history and the public consciousness, they are replete throughout culture, deified in art, prose, and photography (and represented by many a tchotchke such as those that decorate gardens or curio cabinets); gracing stamps and currency; serving as emblems for service organizations and logos for businesses, and headlining advertisements. Portland Head Light, for instance, has been used over the years in promotions for Coca-Cola, Kellogg's, Chevrolet, and IBM—and in one ad campaign a local jeweler even used Photoshop to strap Movado watches around its classic tower.

Throughout Maine and elsewhere, lighthouses ultimately stand as one of humankind's most emblematic structures.

A Grueling Profession

But progress, as they say, doesn't come without suffering.

Those who kept the lights had to deal with harsh, demanding conditions on often secluded, barren isles, sticking it out against the endless clobbering and tempestuous emotions of the wind and sea.

Their duties were vast, rigorous, and relentless, and they lived under stringent rules from the government. Including the tantamount task of maintaining the lights, they were required to keep a daily log of virtually everything that went on at their post (from wind and weather conditions to supply deliveries to the frequency and length of stay of visitors) and perform regimented inspections.

Referring to each other chummily as "wickies," lighthouse keepers were initially politically appointed; the government set rules that those selected were to be between the ages of eighteen and fifty, and had to be literate, able to keep accounts, and adequately perform required manual labor. "Men of intemperate habits" or those "mentally or physically incapable" of doing the job were specifically excluded. (Although many of them were, indeed, men, there were a handful of female light-tenders, one of the most legendary included in the pages to come.)

Ultimately, as outlined by the US Lighthouse Board, which was established in 1852 to provide oversight of stations across the country, keepers were to "consider the care of the light and the light-house property their paramount duty, beyond any personal consideration."

In exchange, they were paid very little, and those at isolated offshore stations—who would often go for months on end without visiting the mainland, and, if they had families, were left to their own devices to school them—were provided with rations of meat and other essentials. But they were not allowed to enhance their paltry salaries by taking on boarders, or selling handcrafted wares or liquor (although many either blatantly ignored this rule or found a way around it).

As they tended their stations, aligning their day-to-day routines with the rhythm of the tides—ever anxious about what the currents could bring—they were witness to the occasional shipwreck, performed valiant rescues, and, ultimately, found ways to forge meaningful and fulfilling lives amidst often trying conditions.

Many Maine lighthouse keepers would write later of the solitude and the punishing nature of the position; but, very often, they would add that they could not foresee any other way of life, noting the profoundly compelling lure of both the lights and the sea.

Keeper Charles L. Knight described this strange dichotomy upon taking up a post at Squirrel Point Light on the Kennebec River.

"It was spring and the warm sunny days had begun. I thought every day was rosy," he recalled, also describing his first year there as a "continued vacation."

However, he added that, "I had no idea what an isolated section I was going into or the hardships I would have to put up with."

It was a unique existence, that, as we shall read, some have simply never been able to leave behind.

Chapter One

Portland Head Light: Dangerous Beauty

What would an ocean be without a monster lurking in the dark?
It would be like sleep without dreams.

—Werner Herzog

It is 1942, the thick of the world's second Great War. The Allies perform an ongoing patrol of the Portland harbor, a key staging port. All is calm and quiet. Fog and thick humidity fall over the area like a shawl.

And then, suddenly, an unmistakable blip appears on the radar.

Primed for action, all hands on deck, naval, Coast Guard, and British boats descend on a location known as Hussey Sound near Peaks Island.

The radar flashes and beeps; the crewmen report the faint silhouette of an unknown vessel upon the waves.

And then, as abruptly as it began, everything stops.

The beeps cease, the crew pauses, the air is once again still. The sea smoke dissipates to reveal not a wake or a wave—or any evidence whatsoever that an enemy ship had been in the area. All that the sailors on the imposing convoy of vessels can see is a tiny rowboat adrift in the water, two terrified, gape-mouthed illicit lovers staring up at them.

Later, that pair (in the area under the cover of mist for a secret rendezvous) offered a version of events that was meant to serve as an explanation—but it only further confounded.

Alarmed by the sudden bluster, they recalled that they looked out across the bay to see the battleships fast in pursuit of a curious-looking boat; it was a masted schooner of the post-Revolutionary days, sails high, hull parting the waves. It passed within yards of them, and, just as it disappeared into the thick fog, they saw that its bow was inscribed with the name "DASH—FREEPORT."

Like most locals, they knew the story of the fabled privateering ship, which had disappeared without even a ripple 130 years before just beyond Portland Head Light, under the same sails but during a different war.

Portland's ghost ship had eluded once more.

The *Dash*, the stuff of both legend and romanticism, is like the Maine version of Odysseus's fated ship: seemingly bound to ride the seas forever seeking port.

It is impossible to talk about Maine lighthouses—or, for that matter, lighthouses in general—without including (and heavily emphasizing) Portland Head Light. The state's first lighthouse commissioned by George Washington and built in 1791, it is one of Maine's most visited landmarks, and stands as the archetype of the modern lighthouse.

With its prototypical white tower and red-shingled outbuildings, it stands guard on the craggy precipice of the Atlantic, rocks just below appearing like layers of petrified wood in their thousands of years enduring the blows and caresses of the sea. It has served as a haven for luminaries such as Henry Wadsworth Longfellow and Harriet Beecher Stowe, and has been immortalized in poem and prose and millions of images: splashed by the dull morning rays of the sun, dyed a myriad of hues in sunset, swathed in mist, dusted with snow, flanked by spring flowers, bracing itself against probing waves as the rocks below it are temporarily swallowed by the ocean.

Today the light is owned by the town of Cape Elizabeth, and sits adjacent to the ninety-acre Fort Williams Park—whose practice fire it bore the brunt of for a time—attracting hundreds of thousands of visitors a year.

As it has stood guard in its various iterations for more than 225 years, the light station has witnessed and amassed a rich history, both earthly and unexplained.

SAILING INTO HISTORY

One of its most legendary stories involves the *Dash*, built (as her name would suggest) for speed in 1813 during America's de facto second revolution. The Freeport-based merchant brothers Sewald and Samuel Porter had her crafted especially for smuggling and eluding. She very quickly developed a reputation for both; on her first maiden run out of Portland to Santo Domingo, in fact, she crossed courses with an established British brig but easily outraced it. Upon her return, her owners were given permission by President James Madison to hunt British ships as a privateer—a bonus being that she could keep all her spoils.

This she did, in all capturing fifteen ships without losing a single crew member.

Until her fateful last voyage in early 1815. Setting sail from Portland, she was met by a new privateer to local waters. Known as the *Champlain* and based out of Portsmouth, New Hampshire, her cocky captain wanted a race.

The *Dash*'s captain, twenty-four-year-old John Porter, was not one to shirk away from such a challenge; so the two set out, very briefly bow to bow.

They were last seen passing the Portland Head Light, the *Dash* easily taking the lead.

However, a tempest soon blew in and the *Champlain* lost sight of its rival before turning back to port.

And that is where the earthly manifestation of the *Dash* sails out of this story. Leaving not a trace of her crew, cargo—or even a scrap of wreckage—she simply disappeared.

Some say she was cursed, her captain, in his haughtiness, not heeding the telltale signs of ill-tidings such as misfiring weapons and bluebirds (said to be harbingers of foul weather).

Nobody knows precisely of her fate; it could be that she capsized while her sails were up in full race mode, or she smashed apart on uncharted land.

Whatever her end, she was mourned by locals and family members of the crew, who were said to habitually make the climb up to the lantern room of Portland Head Light to keep vigil should she one day return.

Which she did—in a way.

Just a few months later, a fisherman working in the Freeport harbor was suddenly swathed in fog; he was undeterred, however, continuing with his duties.

But then he was shocked to a standstill.

Suddenly, a sailing ship with full mast emerged from the cloaked waters, moving forward despite the fact that there was hardly any wind. On its side, its name stood out in bold letters: "DASH—FREEPORT."

Since then, the phantom vessel has been seen sailing all over Casco Bay, off the coast of Freeport, near Harpswell Sound, and around the hundreds of islands that lay splayed along Maine's sizable dominion of the Atlantic.

Some have described her as having tattered sails; others recall her as being in her full regalia of old. In any case, she is seen with a phantom crew standing motionlessly on her decks, face worn-down and left expressionless by an eternity of aimless sailing.

And no matter her condition, she promptly disappears whenever approached, or just as it seems she might collide with land.

Her forlorn tale has been memorialized by both Portland native Henry Wadsworth Longfellow and Harpswell native son Robert P. Tristram Coffin. But perhaps the most well-known homage is John Greenleaf Whittier's "The Dead Ship of Harpswell":

> *For never comes the ship to port,*
> *Howe'er the breeze may be;*
> *Just when she nears the waiting shore*
> *She drifts again to sea.*
> *No tack of sail, nor turn of helm,*
> *Nor sheer of veering side;*
> *Stern-fore she drives to sea and night,*
> *Against the wind and tide.*

LET THERE BE LIGHT

As is the case with many lighthouses (going back to ancient times), Portland Head's installation was a reactionary measure to disaster.

Between 1780 and 1990, at least one hundred vessels were estimated to have wrecked upon the Cape Elizabeth coast, and the locale has long been said to have a superstitious aura for mariners.

One example of the area's treacherous waters occurred on June 26, 1863, when the Civil War's northernmost naval battle was waged just off its shores. Under the cloak of night, Confederate lieutenant Charles W. Read and his crew snuck into Portland and boarded the well-armed US cutter the *Caleb Cushing*. They intended to sail it out of port and then turn it back on the city.

But not long after commandeering the ship, they were betrayed by the harbor's boisterous tides—and were thus easily overtaken and captured by Portland forces.

Locals long clamored for a lighthouse on Cape Elizabeth, growing particularly agitated in February 1787. It was then that a ninety-ton sloop heading south from Sheepscott on the Midcoast wrecked on Cushing Island (located about a mile from where Portland Head Light now stands). The captain and a young boy drowned; the remainder of the crew escaped on floating wreckage.

The following week, the *Cumberland Gazette* demanded, "Does not this unhappy accident evidence the necessity of having a Lighthouse at the entrance of the harbor?"

The light was eventually commissioned by Washington before either the federal government or Maine existed (the state would remain part of Massachusetts until 1820), and was constructed partly of local rubblestone.

Yet Portland Head couldn't quell all catastrophe.

Desperate measures called for it to be raised ninety years later; in February 1864, the *Bohemian*, on its way from Liverpool, broke apart upon its rocks. The 218 passengers and crew escaped in lifeboats; one of those dories, however, was swamped, and forty were drowned.

Humans, in their worst of times, are not much more than vultures or the other scavengers of the animal kingdom—it was said that women from around Casco Bay collected bolts of yarn, wool, satin, and silk that washed ashore after the wreck.

Following the tragedy, the light was raised another twenty feet.

But of all the wrecks it has witnessed over the years, that of the *Annie C. Maguire* in 1886 was perhaps most peculiar.

Just a few days before the disaster, the local sheriff paid a visit to lighthouse keeper Joshua Strout. He foretold of a three-masted schooner headed for Quebec, asking him to keep an eye out for it because it was slated for seizure by American creditors.

Then, on Christmas Eve, a ship bound from Buenos Aires smashed into the ledges off Cape Elizabeth, shaking the lighthouse and keeper's dwelling with the impact.

Reacting quickly, keeper Strout—who, it was said, kept a parrot that warned him when foul weather was ahead—and his son Joseph rigged up emergency lights and a rope chair to haul the crew, captain, and his wife ashore.

Once on dry land, Captain Daniel O'Neil discovered that a satchel that had been on board, holding all the ship's money and papers, was inexplicably missing. Panicked, he whispered to his wife, who advised that he shut up and pretend it had been lost. So the story goes, she had hidden all of its contents inside her hatbox before rescuers hauled her onto land via the rope swing.

Although the sheriff did eventually come by to search the ship, the pair absconded with their take. Its creditors received compensation at auction—but nothing close to the riches that the couple stole.

A classic sepia image of the ship's demise shows the bark, devoid of its sails, lilted sideways and rested upon rocks just below the majestic lighthouse. The wreck is further memorialized with a simple epitaph painted on a rock below the sidewall, first set down in stark black and white by Joseph Strout (listing simply the ship's name and the date).

While no one knows for sure what happened to the captain or her lost treasure, the *Annie C. Maguire* remains one of the most infamous (and puzzling) shipwrecks in Maine history.

GHOSTS, LIGHTS—AND GHOSTLIGHTS

But time, as it steams forward, leaves behind a spiritual wake; one remnant left at Portland Head is said to be the ghost of a boy known as "Little Sam."

Still, even some of the most devout believers in the paranormal say his story amounts to nothing more than that: So it goes, he was the son of a nineteenth-century keeper named Jacob Lancaster—although there is no record of a tender by that name (and we know by now how meticulous and adamant the lighthouse service was about documentation). In any case, it's said, once he grew old enough, the child was supposed to succeed his father; but he never got the chance, dying of typhoid at age twelve.

The years went by, and the old lighthouse keeper grew ill. Finally, during a particularly wicked storm, he was unable to mount the stairs to keep the lantern lit.

Instead, he lay his weary body down in his bed and perished.

Yet the lights shone on. As the man lay dead in the cottage below, his duties were carried on by unseen hands.

Several seamen in the area at the time swore to Davy Jones that they saw the figure of a boy waving at them from the light's iron catwalk—little Sam finally taking over for his doting father? Or perhaps the son of a local resident or mariner, compelled by local tradition from the great beyond?

A lesser-known story involves a figure dressed in dark clothing (similar to a keeper's uniform) seen walking purposefully around the park and the lighthouse. Maybe it is Sam's father, remaining alongside his son in this earthly realm.

Many other unexplainable entities have been witnessed around the light. For instance, in the summer of 1818, just off its shores, a "long beast" was reported by a ship's captain. As he and his crew looked on astonished, the creature raised its head thirty feet out of the water (or so they recalled later to rapt listeners).

Much later, in the 1950s, a fisherman spotted a shape that he estimated to be about one hundred feet long. At first, he assumed it to be a small submarine, and hurried to get out of its path.

Submarines, though, don't dip and dive out of the water so fluidly—or, for that matter, make eye contact.

The fascinated mariner described watching the creature romp for forty-five minutes before it swam off into the fog-blanketed distance.

Meanwhile, in nearby Pond Cove, located just off a pastoral patch of Cape Elizabeth traced with an intaglio of walking trails, a mysterious light is said to reflect an enduring aura of jealousy and betrayal. Flying out of nowhere, it has been described as a pale flaming ball that aggressively dances and dodges.

It was believed to have initially appeared to three fishermen in the early 1900s. As they were rowing into the cove just as dark was descending, the orb suddenly materialized, clearly targeting one of the men, then flying off in the direction of his house.

That very night, the man, seemingly the object of the maliciously darting flash, disappeared, leaving not a scrap of information behind as to why.

Then, twenty years later, long after he was assumed dead, his wife received a letter. Postmarked from an undisclosed location, it was from her long-estranged beau, expressing his love for her and also making a confession. He had committed a murder years before; the man had been a romantic rival vying for her affection shortly before they were married. He killed him so he could have her for his own.

He fled the night the orb came at him, he recounted, believing that it was his victim seeking revenge.

To this day, the light is still seen upon occasion in Pond Cove; vengeful spirits can be hard to quell.

Bright, shiny spheres were also observed in the early 1800s by the clipper ship *Godspeed* upon her return to Portland. As described by author Charles Stansfield, the night was uneventful, with a northeast wind, when suddenly a light came spinning out of the air, bright as can be but soundless. After hovering for what must have seemed like wondrous ages to the onlooking crew, it accelerated once more and disappeared.

Its origins are hard to say—humans have been perplexed since time immemorial by strange lights in the sky.

Shining Just as Brightly

Like an overlord to Maine's largest metropolis, Portland Head Light keeps a careful eye on its namesake city's harbor and surroundings.

Nearby, it has similarly diligent brothers and sisters.

One of the most engaging of those is Ram Island Ledge Light, located in Casco Bay and visible from Portland Head. Its very image instills a feeling of isolation: The tower stands, on its own, jutting forth like a stone exclamation point—or perhaps a comma—from the Atlantic. Illustrating its harsh conditions, it has been captured in photographs with its entire length, stained by the salt and grime of the sea, completely consumed in waves that seem to want to voraciously devour it.

Meanwhile, close by is Cape Elizabeth Two Lights, most iconically rendered by early-twentieth-century painter Edward Hopper. His graceful portrait of its silhouette was even issued on a postage stamp in 1970, the first lighthouse to ever be featured on a US stamp. Its name came from the ever-prolific and enterprising explorer John Smith, and was meant as an honor to the elder sister of King Charles I of England (who would later be beheaded for treason).

One of its decidedly quirky anecdotes involves actor and one-time husband to Bette Davis, Gary Merrill. He purchased the west tower in 1971, and was known to drive around town with his pet donkey in the back of his Cadillac convertible.

As is the case with lighthouses throughout history, the sentinel has gone through much iteration, initially built in 1811 and then, when that structure proved inadequate against the battering of the sea—as well as the increasing boat traffic in Casco Bay—it was refortified with its second tower seventeen years later.

Like Portland Head, it is said to be haunted by a man dressed in dark clothing (again, akin to a tender's uniform); a wily sort, he disappears behind the tower when seen, or, if in more of an engaging mood, stands conspicuously at the end of the keeper's driveway.

There are a few explanations as to his presence.

During the tenure of early keeper Marcus Aurelius Hanna (who was assigned to the post in 1873), for example, a ship's captain perished just moments before he could be rescued.

In January 1885, the schooner *Australia* hit Dyer's Ledge below Two Lights's fog signal. It was the midst of a heavy blizzard, temperatures far below zero.

Hanna, a Civil War sergeant awarded for his heroism in Louisiana (and named after the last of the so-called "Five Good Emperors" of Rome), promptly sprung to action—despite the fact that he had spent the previous few days and nights ill in bed.

The *Australia*, commanded by Captain John W. Lewis, was headed out of Boothbay Harbor to Boston, loaded with ice and barrels of mackerel.

As the ship collided with shore, its three ice-coated crewmen climbed up and clung to its masts.

Hanna's wife saw the ship and felt the tremor as it brusquely met land. Her husband, recuperating from a virus, quickly dressed and ran to shore.

Although it took a few tries, ocean mockingly spraying icy water at him, the keeper landed a line onto the vessel. He then led two of the men to shore, his wife ushering them inside, cutting off their clothes and feeding them hot soup.

The captain, however, wasn't quite so lucky. Although he held fast to the ship as his men were rescued, desperately trying not to let loose his grip as the vessel was dashed to oblivion, the waves proved too strong, consuming him.

For his role in the valiant rescue, Hanna was recognized by the US Life-Saving Service.

Still, that was hardly the end of the troubles for Twin Lights. Another source of the purported ghost could be one-time keeper Joseph Upton.

In 1934, when the main light failed around 9:30 p.m., the sixty-five-year-old climbed the stairs to the tower to activate an auxiliary light. A couple hours later, his wife, startled from sleep, wondered why he had been gone so long. Rushing to the tower, she found him crumpled at the bottom of the staircase, his skull fractured. He was rushed to a Portland hospital, but he soon succumbed to his injuries. Some believe it is his elusive spirit that wanders the lighthouse grounds.

Others, though, have described the very lighthouse itself as a haunting presence.

Captain Frank L. Cotton, who was named head keeper in 1910, wrote of the morose feeling of abandonment that emanated across its shores.

"Lonesome? Well, any man who hasn't put in a good many years on one of those outside lights off the coast of Maine just can't appreciate what that life means," he told author Robert Thayer Sterling in 1925.

Gazing out from his post to the nearby civilization of Portland, he recalled "the brilliant lighted streets and the theaters and the other life other folks of my age were enjoying—well, it did take some grit to stick it out if I do say it."

The lighthouse could be said to possess that very quality; it ceaselessly continues to "stick it out" from its vantage point above the sea.

CHAPTER TWO

The Nubble: Maine's Emblem

Some places speak distinctly. Certain dark gardens cry aloud
for a murder; certain old houses demand to be haunted; certain
coasts are set apart for shipwreck.
—ROBERT LOUIS STEVENSON

IT WAS THE DULL OF DAWN, AN UNRECOGNIZABLE SHORELINE. A plague of horror hung over it; all was silent. Even the gulls were muted and sobered by the scene.

Drifting in the waves, washing into shore, were wooden boxes. No, not just boxes—coffins. Seven of them.

And there was a voice, dank and hollow and dripping with death.

"You will be among them."

The seasoned sailor jolted awake, eyes like discs, breath fast and jagged.

He drifted in the fuzzy twilight between sleeping and waking, the horrible dream still gripping his mind. No, not a dream, a nightmare. Or an omen?

He was scheduled to leave the next morning on the maiden voyage of the *Isidore*, a ship bound from Kennebunkport harbor to the port of New Orleans.

Being a man of the sea, he was devoutly superstitious. He lay awake the rest of the night; the coffins floated at the forefront of his mind as they had in the frozen sea of his dream.

The next morning, still shaken, he told his captain about his nightly horror—which the old salt laughed off with a hearty pat on his back before angrily ordering him to his station.

The man did as he was told, and set to preparing the ship with the other dozen members of the crew. A few hours later, it set sail—never to be seen again.

At least, not in its terrestrial form.

The *Isidore*, which broke to bits on Bald Head Cliff just north of the Nubble in 1842, is a sea tragedy that is the stuff of legend: rife with premonitions and dread and death and unsettled spirits.

Its horrendous wreck prompted officials to investigate erecting a lighthouse on the Nubble, a rocky outcropping just a few hundred feet offshore of Cape Neddick in York—although it was another thirty-five years until the sentinel, one of Maine's most iconic, was to be erected.

Under the direction of thirty-six-year-old Captain Leander Foss, the 396-ton ship *Isidore* pulled up anchor on November 30, 1842, carrying a crew of fifteen and a cargo of lumber.

From the very beginning—nay, as early as the first nails began banging its structure into place—it seemed enshrouded in a cloak of doom. It is only natural for work crews to engage in banter and singing and storytelling, but it was said that the *Isidore* work site was mostly maudlin, gloomy and silent, except for the sounds of hammering and sawing.

Then there were the omens as the day of its launch drew closer and closer. There was the sailor (name since eroded by time) who dreamt of the seven coffins; then there were the similar nightmares of would-be crewman Thomas King. Two nights before the vessel's departure, he literally jumped out of bed upon waking from a terrible dream. In it, he saw a wrecked ship surrounded by bloated corpses. As the lifeless bodies floated in the salty brine, their faces stiffened into stone; a fog suddenly came in not on cat's feet but on lion's paws, snatching away everything except the ship's skeletal hull.

King told Captain Foss of the dream—but much like the vision of the seven coffins, the captain not only laughed it off, but scolded him. Foss was known to be dependable and experienced, not prone to superstition. He had a duty to fulfill, and he expected his crew to do the same. Plus, he had paid every crewmember in advance as a means to ensure they would not worry for their families while they were out at sea for a month.

But once more, King had the dream. This time, his nightly convulsions terrified his young wife—and cemented the young sailor's resolve.

Returning once more to Foss, he begged to be let out of his contract, or at the very least, that the voyage be delayed.

Yet Foss refused to budge, and the ship's departure remained on schedule.

November 30 was said to be dreary and overcast, the air so cold it could crack bones. As the *Isidore* prepared for launch, the crowd watching from the Kennebunkport docks was decidedly subdued. Normally, they would be clamorous and rowdy, but this group didn't put much oomph into their cheering and waving as they saw their friends and family members off.

As some would say later, it seemed much more like an ending than a beginning.

The mood was further dampened when the ship rocked and lilted as it was lowered down its ramp into the sea. However, once it was christened into the waters, it righted itself, to the relief of onlookers.

But as the morning grew into afternoon, the snow began to whip and the air grew even more bitter. As Foss took inventory of his ship and crew, it became clear that one was missing: Thomas King, he with his ridiculous portents.

He had fled his duties, too terrified to board the forsaken ship. Later, it was found out that he hid in the woods until he knew the bark was far out to sea.

The captain and his mates cursed him, but the vessel moved out of the harbor nevertheless under the cloak of snow. Soon, she was lost to view, and the crowd dispersed.

The *Isidore* was last seen passing the lonely, rock-strewn outpost of Boon Island. As the night slowly seized its dominion, the winds and waves and snow became ever more overpowering.

And then, the next morning, came the fateful news: The ship had cracked to bits just off Cape Neddick.

Its hull was in pieces, lumber was floating everywhere, and several bodies had washed ashore—seven, to be precise, including the sailor whose dream had foretold of that very scene.

Captain Foss's body was never recovered, although a stone in Kennebunkport's Village Cemetery bears his name and the inscription:

May this event God sanctify,
And thus prepareus (sic) all to die.
That when we leave this earthly clod,
We may be blessed and dwell with God.

The rest of the retrieved bodies are believed to be buried in common, unmarked graves.

As for those who were never found? It is said they are prescribed to sail the seas for eternity.

Not long after the wreck, reports started circling about a mysterious ship resembling the *Isidore*. Mariners who have claimed to have witnessed it have described a phantom boat manned by a crew of gaunt men dressed in tattered rags, their faces blank, eyes empty. They appear shadowy and stand motionless, staring straight ahead, their ship soundlessly guiding itself. It's been said that, when attempts are made to address or approach the mysterious vessel, it abruptly turns and sails off in the opposite direction, or altogether disappears.

Some say the ill-fated men sail on as a warning; others believe they are endlessly seeking out Thomas King, the mate who deserted them.

Whatever their reasons, their lore endures.

The stories may be rejected as superstition, or a product of "morbid imagination," reporter Chandler Briggs Allen wrote in the *Maine Sunday Telegram* in a story commemorating the tragedy in 1912 (coincidentally or not, the same year the "unsinkable" RMS *Titanic* ended up scattered along the floor of the north Atlantic). However, he continued, even the "hardest headed person" must accept "well-substantiated and incontrovertible facts.

"There are enough to make one wonder if, after all, there might not be a grain of truth in the yarn the sailors used to tell," he contended.

Indeed, we can only wonder if the doomed ship still sails on, a bath toy to Poseidon's whims.

Out of This World
Had the Nubble lighthouse been in place in 1824, as locals had lobbied for decades, the tragedy might have been thwarted. Or perhaps the sailors, facing the same brutal weather, would have wrecked elsewhere, sailing off into another legend.

But as history has taught us, the breadcrumb trails of "what-ifs" are fruitless and endless ones.

Before being bestowed with its current name—"nubble" meaning "small knob" or "lump"—the roughly two-and-a-half acre island was known as "Savage Rock." The name came from English explorer Captain Bartholomew Gosnold, who held a parlay with Indians there in 1602.

As recounted by the ship's historian, John Brereton, the natives were naked, save for deer skins about their shoulders and seal skins around their waists. Being "swart" in color, they were "strong and well-proportioned," with hair tied in knots and paint adorning their bodies.

"They spoke diverse Christian words," he recalled, "and seemed to understand much more than we, for want of language to comprehend."

A largely barren, jagged hump that juts forth out of the Atlantic, the island has long been distinguished for its characteristic rock formations, which have been chiseled away over millennia. From the air, its craggy outcroppings appear to hold the sea in a tight, imposing grip.

Among those is the legendary "Devil's Oven," a dangerous precipice with a fifty-foot drop, and "Washington's Rock," where visitors and locals alike have claimed to see the face of the nation's first president.

The lighthouse was finally put into service in July 1879. It consists of a forty-foot white brick tower standing ninety-two feet above the sea, accompanied by a quaint red-roofed keeper's house (and two other pitched-roof outbuildings).

Thirty-two cast iron spiral steps and a ship's ladder lead to the lantern room, which overlooks the craggy, wave-tossed outline of York Harbor. (Because of its perilous rocks, many keepers were said to have tied their children to posts, or the lighthouse ladder, to ensure they didn't wander off and hurt themselves.)

But beyond the disquieting apparitions of the *Isidore* and its fated crew, the lighthouse and island are said to be imbued with a positive, infectious spirit.

Local author and historian Bill Thomson calls this Nubble's "happy ghost."

It has "something in the air," he told seacoastonline.com in 2009. "People come here with minor problems, sit here, their problem(s) (are) solved."

Indeed, it is one of the few stations in the state that many lighthouse keepers have been reluctant to leave, and the town of York has wholeheartedly embraced it as its own.

Today, the lighthouse is one of the most photographed in Maine; hundreds of thousands of people visit its home at Sohier Park every year.

Keepers over the years have cashed in on its popularity, charging money for tours and ferries across from the mainland—very often getting themselves in trouble with the Lighthouse Board. Others, meanwhile, were disquieted or outright maddened by the attention; Coast Guard Keeper Russ Ahlgren said existing with camera-bearing tourists just a few hundred feet away was like "living in a fish bowl looking out at the rest of the world."

The Nubble is so emblematic, in fact, that its digitized image was included in the "Golden Record" of the Voyager II space probe, which was sent out in 1977 to explore the outer planets of our solar system (and potentially discover alien life). The spacecraft's Record, among other things, was etched with 115 images, including those of the Taj Mahal and the Great Wall of China. The Nubble was chosen to represent the seashore, and, thus, humankind's preferred proximity to water, according to

Jon Lomberg, the Record's design director. The waves could help extraterrestrials deduce details about our planet's gravity, atmospheric composition, and surface pressure, he added.

"But the handsome, rugged shore of Maine is a fitting snapshot of the beauty of our planet, whatever else it says," he told Smithsonian.com.

In that case, perhaps the *Isidore* has made it as far as space, its doomed sailors serving as a warning to other unearthly souls?

CHAPTER THREE

Boon Island: Stranded by Fate

I want to marry a lighthouse keeper and keep him company.
I want to marry a lighthouse keeper and live by the side of the sea.
—ERIKA EIGEN

DRESS CRUMPLED AND STREAKED WITH BLOOD, HAIR TANGLED and snarled, eyes swollen and red and exhausted of tears, the young woman climbed the winding stairs with pained, halting steps.

At the top, she dragged herself into the small lantern room. Moving with routine, mechanical gestures that seemed led by the hands of another, she cut the wicks on the lanterns and then refilled them with oil.

She took a second to glance out over the ocean: It was a vast, black nothingness indiscernible from the equally dark sky.

Then she descended the tower's 168 steps—to her beloved.

He lay in a heap at the base of the stairs, his body, having been overtaken and then tossed about by the cruel sea, stiffening and decaying.

She resumed her spot beside his frozen corpse, listening to the wind screeching and battering the granite structure, begging to be let in. She didn't want to eat, didn't want to sleep; she just wanted her dear Lucas back.

Endless Love

When they found Katherine Bright nearly a week later, she was on the edge of hypothermia, starved, babbling, and incoherent, cradling her lover's limp body.

Guided by duty, she had kept Boon Island's guiding light burning for five days during a battering storm after her husband had perished in the grip of the ocean's frigid waters.

But exhaustion and grief finally took over—and the untended light waned, then died out.

Local fishermen came to investigate, only to find a grisly, heartbreaking sight.

They quickly shuttled the delirious widow and her husband's corpse back to the mainland. It was said that Katherine went mad and died in a hospital soon thereafter.

But many believe she never truly left.

Over the years, keepers, mariners, and visitors have reported seeing the ghostly figure of a woman in white making her way along the rocky ledges near the lighthouse. Other times, some claim, she has been so bold as to knock at the keeper's dwelling—and when the door is answered, her apparition is seen flitting toward the tower.

In a few instances, keepers have attested that the tower light has mysteriously been lit or kept brightened by unseen hands. Then there have been unexplained footsteps, and, even more eerily, mournful cries and screeches heard as far away as the mainland.

Animals—as has been said throughout time—have been particularly sensitive to her purported presence. Keepers' cats and dogs have avoided or simply refused to enter the lighthouse tower; some canines have been seen running up and down the island, barking madly, chasing something unseen by human eyes.

Could it be Katherine, a grieving wife forever bound by duty, keeping watch over the isle and its light?

Her legend goes back to the mid-1800s. It was then that young lighthouse keeper Lucas Bright (name seemingly all too fitting for his profession) brought her to live with him at his station at Boon Island.

Initially, they were happy, spending a pleasant four months keeping house, tending to the lights, and enjoying the ocean air and each other's company.

But then winter set in—a dread for many a New Englander, but especially punishing for lighthouse keepers.

One evening, a particularly unpleasant gale roared over the coast. Lucas, both fearing for the island's only boat and frantic to keep the light going, set out into the storm, despite the pleadings of his wife. As a means of safety, he tied himself to the lighthouse, gave Katherine a kiss, and braced himself against the battering winds and spraying surf.

But as helpless Katherine watched, he was overtaken by a giant wave; it swept up over the island and dragged him into the icy sea, drowning him and smashing his lifeless body against the ragged rocks.

Summoned with strength, his young wife hauled and hefted his body in, fighting against the inexorable pull of the sea. She dragged him to the lighthouse, collapsing with him at the base of the stairs—heartbroken, terrified, alone.

But as we have seen, lighthouse keepers are a devoted and conscientious sort, so despite her anguish, feelings of helplessness, deteriorating physical and mental state—not to mention the inevitable shock—she knew she had to keep the light going so that others would not suffer the same horrible fate.

Surviving on nothing but sheer will, every few hours she dutifully climbed over her husband's body and up the tower stairs to ensure the lights kept burning. Otherwise, she never left dead Lucas's side—though his body was mangled, frozen and discolored, and rigor mortis was setting in.

She continued like this for five days, until the fuel was nearly diminished and she became too weak to climb the stairs.

As she lay, close to death herself, with her husband, the light slowly dimmed, flickered, then flared out.

With the tower plunged in darkness, temperatures plummeted, eventually dropping below zero.

One can only wonder the young widow's thoughts in that pitch black, frozen, howling madness. It must have seemed endless and blinding, hope and feeling snuffed out with the light.

But all storms come to an end; when this one ceded to calmer fronts, concerned fishermen from York landed on the island and were shocked to find the incapacitated woman clinging desperately to a corpse.

Nineteenth-century poet Celia Laighton Thaxter wrote of the lovers' sorrowful end in the poem "The Watch of Boon Island":

> They found her watching, silent, by her dead,
> A shadowy woman, who nor wept, nor wailed,
> But answered what they spake, till all was said.
> They bore the dead and living both away.
> With anguish time seemed powerless to destroy
> She turned, and backward gazed across the bay,
> Lost in the sad sea lay her rose of joy.

A Boon for Disaster

Yet the tragedy of the young lovers is just one of the many chapters in Boon Island's grisly history book.

Beyond countless natural calamities, shipwrecks, and drownings, another legend involves the *Increase*, a trading vessel that dashed upon its shores in 1682. The four surviving sailors toughed it out on the island for an entire month, living on what food they could find, mostly fish and pilfered gulls eggs. They were finally rescued when natives from the mainland spotted smoke from their fire and rowed out in their boats to investigate.

Since then, there have been reported instances of phantom fires: They are said to erupt out of nowhere and just as suddenly disappear, leaving no evidence such as ash or embers or burn scarring.

Some credit those shipwrecked sailors for the island's name; upon rescue, they were said to have called it boon, for "lucky place." Others, however, attribute the title to quite the opposite—a gruesome case of cannibalism in the 1700s (of which we will read shortly) that spawned a tradition by fishermen to leave emergency rations on the island for any unlucky enough to be stranded in the future. (However, it was called either "Boone," or, more fittingly because of its ghastly history, "Bone," much earlier by settlers including John Winthrop.)

The island's very location and landscape seem to set the scene for horror and heartbreak. The tiny spot of land—spanning just three hundred by seven hundred feet at low tide, and located six-and-a-half miles off Maine's southern coast—has been described as barren—perched barely 10 feet above the high water mark, shrubless, treeless, soil not fertile enough for even the simplest of gardens.

"It nowhere shows the smallest part of natural soil," William C. Williams, keeper for twenty-seven years beginning in 1885, told author Robert Thayer Sterling. "It is hardly an island."

Yet it is home to Maine's tallest lighthouse, originally built in 1812—and rebuilt in 1831, and then again in 1855. Seen from a distance, the slim gray structure is striking in its height, appearing like a giant medieval tower. Dark, ominous, unwelcoming, streaked black with years of brine, it seems a darker cousin to the picturesque Maine lighthouses that come to mind.

Those who have spent time tending it have described its sheer desolation.

Young Annie Bell Hobbs, in the January 1876 issue of the children's magazine *Nursery*, described Boon Island as an outcropping of rock surrounded by the broad imposing Atlantic, "upon which I have been a prisoner, with the privilege of the yard, the past two years."

The fourteen-year-old, daughter of assistant keeper Edwin Hobbs, continued: "Now and then sails dot the wide expanse, reminding me that there is a world besides the little one I dwell in, all surrounded by water."

Williams also spoke of its isolation and the ocean's cruel devastation. Carrier pigeons were at times the only means of communication, soil had to be brought in from the mainland in buckets to create even the most meager of gardens (which were most often swept away by waves), and up in the sparse lantern room, the only seat was an upturned box.

During violent storms the sea would completely overtake it, bashing down doors, flooding structures, and carrying away anything movable: giant boulders, hen coops, boardwalks. The tower swayed in brutal winds—which, as they howled through, created eerie sounds like "mad music from an Aeolian harp."

Williams also recalled bizarre instances in which disoriented birds and ducks flew into the tower during storms—sometimes so many that they could be picked up by the bushel.

"There were days when I first went to the station that I could not get away from the idea that I was the same as locked up in a cell," Williams said. "It was a funny experience to be on a place and know you couldn't get off if you wanted to."

A GRUESOME LEGACY

That sentiment is but a whisper of the sheer desperation of a crew shipwrecked on Boon in 1710.

That year, Captain John Deane sailed his 120-ton *Nottingham Galley* out of London toward the colonies. Almost immediately, he ran into a spate of bad weather; for more than eighty days, the sailors couldn't make out anything, in any direction, on the horizon.

Then, during a particularly ruthless blizzard on the dark night of December 11, the Galley finally found land: It abruptly cracked apart on the ragged ledges of Boon Island.

Deane and thirteen members of his crew survived. The captain later wrote that they were "joyful" to be alive, thanking "Providence for their deliverance."

That joy, however, was undoubtedly short-lived, if not instantly fleeting.

The crew hastily used pieces of the foremast to crawl across, escaping the frigid waters to the island. They then created a makeshift tent from remnants of the sail.

Beyond that, they were left with nothing: All the wreckage from the ship quickly washed away in the bitter winds and surf.

Although they could spot Portsmouth Harbor and saw ships on the horizon, there was no dry wood on the island for them to kindle a fire as a means of a signal—or, just as importantly, for warmth.

The only food was the meager pickings they could gather (mussels, captured birds, shellfish, seaweed); the only water the melting snow around them. It wasn't long before they became gaunt, weak, eyes hollowed and empty, clothes and flesh hanging from their frozen and exhausted bones. In a rather brutal bout of irony, the ship's cook was the first to succumb to the situation and the elements.

The rest of the survivors huddled together for warmth, but that didn't keep frostbite from gnawing away at their fingers and toes; there was nothing they could do but deal with the bitter agony and roaring pain as their extremities began to turn black and fall off.

As the days turned into weeks, who can describe their desperation and despair? How many began to court insanity on that isolated isle, or hallucinate on account of malnutrition? How many wished they had surrendered a quick death to the sea, rather than enduring this slow, torturous anguish as they literally became ghosts?

Two of their number, frenzied in their isolation, managed to craft a crude boat—so crude that almost as soon as they launched it, it was broken up by the roiling surf, and the two men were never seen by their shipmates again. The body of one washed ashore (eventually prompting a rescue); his companion was never found.

Finally, completely beyond hope, propelled by the instinct to survive, they resorted to one of the most tabooed practices known to humans: cannibalism.

At the end of December, the ship's carpenter succumbed to the cold clawed fingers of death. As Captain Deane later described him, he was "a fat man, naturally of a dull, heavy, phlegmatick (*sic*) constitution, and aged about 47."

The following morning, the men moved his corpse a distance away from their "camp"—but the enticement of any available kind of meat, even human, was too great.

The starving sailors took a vote: Would they, or would they not, eat the body of their dead shipmate?

The majority agreed.

They sliced his body apart, feeding their aching bellies with his raw flesh.

Deane described the sickening practice.

"A few thin slices, wash'd in salt-water, were brought into the tent, and given to every one, with a good quantity of Rockweed to supply the place of bread," he wrote. The first piece (which he himself ate) was "part of the gristles that compose the breast, having the flesh scrap'd clean off."

He acknowledged that he and others "abominated the loathsome diet," although his "importunate appetite" had led him to the unthinkable, such as surveying "with a longing eye the extremities of his fore fingers."

The mate and two others refused to partake in the flesh-eating that night—but the next morning, constitution completely consumed by hunger, they were the first to "beg an equal share in the common allowance."

The stranded men continued like this for days on end, mutilating the body of their one-time companion.

Then, finally, after twenty-three days on the island, they were rescued on January 2, 1711. A crew from York came to investigate after the body of one of the raft-makers washed ashore.

The rescuers were appalled by what they found: Men who were barely stick figures; delirious, frozen, forced by fate into the outright macabre.

The crew returned to London, still in shock from their ordeal, many with physical ailments they would live with to their last days—and perhaps beyond that. But Deane, the shameless self-promoting type, was quick to publish a story about the wreck that portrayed him as the swarthy hero. It soon became a bestseller.

It was quickly followed up by a conflicting account by the mate, the boatswain, and another of the crew. Their version charged that the captain was ornery and abusive, going so far as to beat some crewmembers so severely that they became crippled (and it was said that years later he accidentally killed his own brother). They surmised that the shipwreck was part of an evil master plan: Deane was desperate for the ship's insurance money, so he had intended to betray it to the French, or have it overtaken by pirates, driving it into waters known to be frequented by them. When neither of those attempts worked, they believed he purposely crashed it into Boon.

But whatever the cause, the pure morbidity of those three weeks left a dark, enduring imprint on both the men and the island.

Pained moans and anguished sighs are said to drift over the isle's jagged, rocky landscape. Visitors, meanwhile, have described the intense and unmistakable sensation that they're being watched. Sometimes the feeling is accompanied by the sound of lurching footfalls approaching in the darkness, then shuffling away before their bearer can be seen or addressed.

Then there are the chilling stories of the ghosts of emaciated, expressionless sailors, clothes disintegrated to rags, who suddenly materialize out of nothing; they simply stare forlornly at those who glimpse them before disappearing once again into the mist.

Most likely, they are the distressed souls of the shipwrecked survivors, eternally unsettled by their own conscience, forever paying the price for their grisly, unthinkable acts.

CHAPTER FOUR

Wood Island: Isle of Misfortune

So many horrid ghosts.
—SHAKESPEARE, *HENRY V*

ON THE MORNING OF JUNE 2, 1896, THE *BIDDEFORD DAILY JOURNAL* announced a vicious murder-suicide with a headline almost poetic in its prose:

SHOT ANOTHER, THEN HIMSELF

Murder and Suicide at Wood Island Yesterday.
Repeating Rifle the Weapon.
Howard Hobbs killed Frederick W. Milliken.
Bullet in his own Brain.
Liquor Mainly Responsible For The Tragedy.

It was a bloody, impulsive incident that stunned and confounded Wood Island's handful of residents—including esteemed lighthouse keeper Thomas Orcutt—as well as inhabitants of the villages that lay within sight on the mainland.

But heart-rending and grisly as it was, some say it was just one in a sinister pattern of events that have plagued the thirty-five-acre island for as far back as locals can remember (and perhaps long before).

Mariners have long been suspicious of the small spot of land just offshore of Biddeford Pool, pointing to the countless ships and sailors that have been swallowed up along its banks—not to mention various occurrences that defy explanation. Some even say that a jinx has been placed on the "barren bit of terra firma" (suggesting quite the converse of its name), according to author Robert Thayer Sterling.

Its classically New England lighthouse, a white tower standing forty-four feet and attached to a humble keeper's dwelling, was put into service in 1808 as a means to help quell maritime disasters.

Its presence, however, could do nothing to prevent tragedies of a different sort.

FATAL DRINK

He was saturated with rum; late on his rent (in fact, he had never once paid it); and had narrowly avoided being locked up the previous evening.

Imbued and emboldened with drink, returning from a bout of debauchery at nearby Old Orchard Beach, the last thing twenty-four-year-old Howard Hobbs needed was a confrontation.

But that's just what he got.

Hobbs was a fisherman who, it was said, devoted as much time to finding oblivion in a bottle as he did to the sea. He lived in a converted hennery owned by his landlord Frederick Milliken that, according to the *Biddeford Daily Journal*, was "rather uninviting"—but as he and his roommate Moses "cared little for external appearances and the luxuries of life, the place made fairly comfortable quarters for them."

Milliken, meanwhile, was thirty-five, married, a special officer, game warden, lobsterman, fisherman—and all-around hard-working man. Some called him a giant, and one story is that he was so strong that he could carry a small boat upon his shoulders. He owned two sets of buildings that were the only structures (besides the lighthouse buildings) on the southern end of Wood Island.

On the afternoon of Hobbs's return, it was a beautiful day just on the cusp of summer.

As he tipsily rowed back to the island with Moses, Milliken, taking advantage of the nice weather, was working outside with his son.

The two young men set ashore around 4:30; as they dragged their dory out of the water, Milliken approached.

Hobbs agreed to talk—but only after retrieving a .42-caliber repeating rifle from his shack.

Concerned, Milliken fetched his police badge.

When the two met once again outside, the landlord asked his young renter if the weapon was loaded—a question that was met with a retort and a slurred laugh.

Perhaps underestimating Hobbs's imbibed state of mind, Milliken then approached him, reaching for the gun.

That was when Hobbs raised it—and shot the man point blank.

Moses and Milliken's wife stood by in horror; they had no time to react. Mortally wounded, Milliken ambled in agony, clutching his side as blood seeped through his clothing and spattered onto the ground. Leaving a crimson trail behind them, the two onlookers helped the dying man inside, easing him onto the bed. Moses then ran off to shore, quickly rowing to the mainland to fetch a doctor.

Hobbs, meanwhile, stood by wide-eyed and quiet, seemingly sobered up from the shock and recognition of what he'd done. Finally, he offered to help—but still apparently "frenzied," according to news reports, he threatened to shoot Milliken's wife when she begged him to surrender the gun.

As she pleaded for him to confess the crime to lighthouse keeper Orcutt, he babbled and sputtered that it was all Milliken's fault; if he'd just left him alone, none of this would have happened.

Eventually, some part of him appealed to reason; he walked, resigned in purpose, to the lighthouse, where the increasingly alarmed Orcutt listened to his story.

Then the young man returned to his shack.

Just a few minutes later, a single shot reverberated like an exclamation point through the otherwise tranquil afternoon.

Finally, someone went to investigate; Hobbs's body was found in his sleeping loft, blood pouring out of a self-inflicted wound. The rifle lay beside him. The fatal bullet had passed through his head and lodged into the wall, "so deeply that it was just discernible from the surface," as reported by the *Daily Journal*.

Nearby, there was a hastily written goodbye note, as well as a sealed letter; he requested that it be delivered to a woman onshore that he had been courting.

It wasn't long before authorities and physicians descended; the usually quiet island was atwitter with activity.

Following an autopsy, it was determined that Milliken died after the bullet entered his abdomen, struck a rib, and lodged into his liver.

The *Daily Journal* wrote of his sudden widow: She "bore the shock of the killing of her husband before her very eyes, with remarkable fortitude." The whole time the authorities were on the island she "showed great calmness and patience."

Qualities, that, had Hobbs possessed them, might have prevented the horrible murder.

TRAGEDY ENDURES

But the killing is just one of the many misfortunes that Wood Island has been host to.

Another story involves a hermit who took up residence on the island not too long after the aforementioned episode; he chose a decrepit old building for his home, surviving by fishing and catching lobster.

But, as John Donne observed, "no man is an island"; loneliness quickly overtook him, and when he grew bored of his self-imposed solitary confinement, he traveled to the mainland and rented a hotel room in the seaside city of Saco.

The next morning, conceivably despondent at the thought of returning to his lonely existence, he forfeited this life and leaped out the hotel window.

But some say he returned nevertheless; an apparition resembling him—as noted by the very few who actually made his acquaintance—is said to pace impatiently up and down the shore near the building he temporarily called his home.

Yet another disastrous circumstance involves a French bootlegger who purportedly set up shop on the island around the same time. He sold liquor to the many fishing crews that sailed by or anchored offshore.

One night, a group of sailors partied hard along its shores; as can often happen during such drunken revelry when there is no shortage of rum, brawls were rampant and mob mentality took over.

Someone made the suggestion that they burn down the bootlegger's shack. It was promptly taken up. The crowd cheered and hooted as the hungry flames engulfed the small quarters.

But fire is one of Mother Nature's few tricks that can't be controlled—it raged in its fury, spreading to the nearby outbuilding where the bootlegger kept his alcohol. An explosion wasn't far behind; the night sky was soon "brilliant with blue flames," according to Robert Thayer Sterling, that could purportedly be seen from twenty miles away.

Today? Some say you can still see it burning from time to time, a phantom remnant of that night.

There have been numerous other mysterious manifestations along Wood Island's shores and in its lighthouse and accompanying buildings.

Doors are said to bang shut on their own (when there is no wind to speak of), window shades spool and unspool themselves, and gunshots have been heard reverberating across the island when no one has been known to be in the vicinity.

In a startling close encounter, the wife of a former keeper was rummaging in a closet and suddenly bumped into something that she wasn't at all expecting—what she identified as a male spirit.

The breadths and depths of the lighthouse have also been plumbed by paranormal investigators.

They have reported swooping black shadows, strange dancing green lights and disembodied music, and mediums in their group have claimed to have encountered the sobbing spirit of a woman who said she was killed by an Indian; a pirate deserted by his ship-mates; and a ghost who insisted that three girls had been held captive in a shack that once stood on the island, then were murdered and buried. Ghost hunters have also allegedly caught the image of a female apparition appearing as a glowing mass of light, and recorded ethereal voices saying, "I think the shot got them!"

In another instance, a medium, while up in the lantern room, said her body was overtaken by the spirit of a man, and kept repeating the phrase, "I didn't mean to do it . . . I didn't mean to do it. . . ."

Could that be Hobbs's mournful spirit, attempting to atone for his crime?

"Oh there are ghosts here," Ron Kolek of the New England Ghost Project told the *Boston Globe* during a paranormal probe of the property in 2005. "Can't you feel them?"

Another anecdote adds to Wood Island's lore: When it was once slated for demolition, it was even briefly considered for a nuclear testing site—which no doubt would have ratcheted up the intensity of paranormal activity. (Can anyone say radioactive ghosts?)

CAREFREE IN SPIRIT

A much less sinister legend emanates from the lighthouse on nearby Goat Island, just a few nautical miles southwest. Since keeper Dick Curtis drowned in a boating accident on Memorial Day in 1992, locals and keepers have sworn they've seen his apparition in the keeper's house. Sightings have sometimes been accompanied by ongoing mechanical problems—such as the heat turning on and off on its own—the island's fog horn sounding when no one is there to ring it, and items being mischievously rearranged.

Meanwhile, the isle seems to be host to its own fog bank: It blows in and completely blankets it, even when the rest of the area is free and clear.

Those who knew Curtis say all these occurrences are hallmarks of his congenial demeanor.

Chapter Five

Seguin Island: Deadly Melody

A man kills the thing he loves, and he must die a little himself.
—Clive Barker

It was intolerable; the infernal melody played over and over and over again, never ceasing.

The repeating notes permeated his brain, clouding his thoughts—even when he was out on the island beyond earshot of the house, or up in the isolation of the light tower where the lanterns held their constant vigil. And sleep was no refuge; in his dreams the music relentlessly played on and on.

He just couldn't take it anymore.

Retrieving an ax, he entered the front door, crossing to the threshold of the parlor.

There she was, a permanent fixture perched at the piano, banging away at the horrid instrument. The same piece in a constant loop. The only one she could—or would—play.

Consumed by anger and frustration, he raised the ax and roared across the room.

The blade slashed down, splintering wood, severing strings, sending ivory keys pinging off the walls. Errant, discordant notes sounded like final death throes.

He paid no attention to his wife's terrified, anguished screams as she watched the violent destruction. All he could think was that he was finally, blissfully, blotting out that nightmare of sound.

Within minutes, the piano was a mere pile of rubble. The house was quiet, the blessed silence he craved.

He turned to his wife. She was wide-eyed, face contorted in horror, screams weakened to yelps.

Something in him—a flinch of madness—made him raise the ax once more.

He brought it down upon her.

Again.

And again.

And again.

This brutal murder, purportedly taking place in the mid-1800s on the secluded sixty-four-acre Seguin Island, is one of the most legendary in not only Maine's lighthouse history—but all of lighthouse history.

Commissioned in 1795 by George Washington himself, Seguin is Maine's second-oldest lighthouse, located off the Midcoast hamlet of Georgetown and about a mile-and-a-half south of where the Kennebec River melds with the Atlantic. Standing 186 feet above water, it provides the highest focal plane of any of Maine's lighthouses.

Its name is believed to be a bastardization of the Abenaki word "sutquin," or "satquin," which translates to the rather unbecoming, "the place where the sea vomits." Others claim that it stands for "hump." French explorer Samuel de Champlain, meanwhile, called its expanse reminiscent of a tortoise (which, when examined in aerial photographs, seems quite an apt description).

Whatever the interpretation, Seguin is known to be one of the foggiest places in the country (one year, for instance, its fog signal rang for 2,734 hours—ultimately three months when all put together); it can be whipped by wind and tide from opposite directions; and it is located near a magnetic disturbance that disorients sailors by setting their compasses spinning.

The experience of the area's first colonists (indeed, some of the first Europeans to settle North America itself) should have served as a warning.

In 1607, English settlers anchored two ships at the island before debarking on the shoreline near the Kennebec. They began to build a town there that they called "Popham"—but gave up within just a year, setting sail for the comfort of home.

Seguin's prone setting wreaked havoc on its lighthouse from the very beginning; originally constructed of wood, the onslaught of swiping seas and winds had nearly destroyed it within just two decades' time. It was reconstructed of stone in 1819 and outfitted with a new keeper's dwelling and a fog bell. (Although, it should be noted, the Atlantic didn't cease its battering; it was rebuilt once more in 1857.) Its compound also includes an oil house, boathouse, and donkey barn.

Among other strange occurrences around the light and its environs, it's said that the vibrations from its fog bell are so strong that it knocks seagulls out of the air and snuffs lanterns straight out. Meanwhile, its bright Fresnel lens—today the only first-order Fresnel lens operating in Maine—has also said to be a calamity for birds.

One-time keeper and assistant keeper Captain Herbert L. Spinney, who also happened to be an amateur ornithologist, commented on the erratic avian behavior:

"It was the light that drew many of the birds . . . comparatively few were killed by striking the plate glass around the light directly, but many, seeing the light, flew in an arc upward, hitting the top of the light [that] they could not see. Many were killed this way, and the next morning . . . 500 or more lay at the base of the light and many more at a greater distance."

Another unique characteristic of Seguin is its roughly one-thousand-foot tramway motored by a hoisting engine installed in the nineteenth century. It connected the boathouse to the keeper's house, aiding in the transport of both people and supplies. However, when it went careening out of control in the 1940s, nearly ejecting a family and decapitating their dog, it was deemed no longer fit for human passengers—yet its weather-worn skeleton still stands today.

While various improvements helped to make Seguin more habitable and better fortify it against the wicked weather, it did nothing to salve the desolation of those who lived there.

JUST CAN'T GET IT OUT OF YOUR HEAD

As the story goes, it was to the bleak environment of Seguin that a new lighthouse keeper (name long forgotten, lost, or, as some say, never was) brought his young wife in the mid-nineteenth century.

Although the keeper himself was mild-mannered and country-bred, his bride was said to be cosmopolitan, the type who thrived amid bustle and the presence of others—so it wasn't long before loneliness and boredom set in for the young woman. She never got to see her friends or family, and there was little stimulation on the island beyond the native wildlife or the flora and fauna tossed in by the surf.

Determined to keep her happy, her husband purchased a piano on the mainland, which he had shipped over on a raft. It was then hoisted up the steep, quarter-mile-long embankment to the keeper's house, where it was placed in the parlor.

She of course was pleased with the present, and, although she could read music but was not a trained piano player, began tinkering with it day and night.

But there was an immediate issue with the music—in that there was only one sheet for her to read from. Some versions of the story say that that was all the instrument came with, and the hapless husband had not thought to purchase more. Others contend that, while the piano was being lifted up to the island, the seat of its bench—where pianists store their scores—fell open, tossing all but one precious sheet into the sea.

But there being just one melody was no matter to her: She played it, replayed it, and soon learned it by heart.

Morning, afternoon, and night she repeated the same song, lulled by the music, notes quelling her otherwise drab and boring life on the godforsaken isle.

The keeper found it endearing at first, touched by how much she cherished his gift. But the repetition soon grated on him.

"Please play something else," he prodded her. "Learn another tune?"

But she wouldn't stop, even as he began to beg, then demand, that she do so.

Had she gone mad? (Why her husband didn't return to the island to procure more sheet music is one of the most enduring questions of this story.)

Finally, he'd had enough. He snapped, grabbed an ax, and sliced the piano apart as his wife was in mid-song (or rather mid-song, mid-song, mid-song). Yet he didn't stop there, and the reasons why are questions lost to time and only known to him—he turned the weapon on his terrified wife, chopping her to pieces.

Not long after, the keeper then killed himself, either by brutal suicide with the murderous maul, a gun, a noose, or via a headlong plunge into the sea (depending on the teller of the tale).

But even sweet death couldn't make the music stop.

Subsequent keepers and visitors have reported hearing phantom piano notes drifting across the island—although no one can quite name the tune. It's even said to reach as far as distant boats or the mainland on the occasion of a calm, windless night.

Still others have seen the specter of the murderous keeper himself, appearing alone on the shoreline, up in the light tower, or among clusters of visitors. When glimpsed, he is splattered with blood, still clutching his axe.

The lady herself has also been thought to wander the cliffs, perhaps forever in despair over her husband's sheer brutality, as well as her ruined instrument.

While some refute the story's validity—there are no known published reports of a murder-suicide at Seguin, and conspiracy theories involve cover-ups or a homicidal intruder—the legend persists.

Much like the tortured wife's never-ending melody.

Seguin's Other Drifting Notes

But beyond the story of the murderous keeper, Seguin is abundant with tales of the spectral, the unnatural, and the outright unexplainable.

To start, serpents have been glimpsed off its depths. In one instance, in July 1875, for example, a captain and his one-man crew were sailing around the island's stony ledges. Suddenly, appearing out of nowhere, there was a "monster" that they estimated to be 130 feet long.

Before they could react, it put its head—the size of a hogshead, according to a report in the *Morning Sentinel*—over the rail; the captain said he attacked it with a pike, scaring it away. The same captain returned to shore with "detritus" from the animal still stuck on the sharp forks of his weapon.

In another instance, a steamer reported coming within thirty feet of a strange creature. "The monster was lazily floating along the water when sighted, occasionally lifting its head to look around, and appeared to be making itself at home in that vicinity," the *Morning Sentinel* reported, adding wryly that the creature was probably engaged in a comprehensive survey of the coast.

Meanwhile, the island is rumored by some to be the final resting place of Captain Kidd and his mistress Anne Bonney; age-old stories circulate that they deposited their treasure on Seguin while on the run from authorities. But as with many pirate tales, this one has never been corroborated, and it mirrors stories of many of Maine's islands—almost all of which are believed to house some or another pirate's treasure.

A ghost known as the "Old Captain" is also said to claim Seguin as his own.

He has been seen, and his footsteps have been heard, climbing the tower to the lamp. And he isn't at all shy about his presence; rather, he's quite brash. He's said to move and replace tools, arrogantly sweep coats and caps off hooks onto the floor, and rearrange various items to his liking.

For instance, according to the Friends of Seguin Light Station—which helps to maintain and improve the lighthouse and its grounds—the caretakers' log for Jack and Tobi Graham chronicled an oval platter exploding on the morning of July 14, 2005. As they recorded, it was just sitting there nondescriptly; then out of nowhere, it completely shattered.

In other instances, the captain's silhouette has been seen working inside when no human was known to be present.

Some believe the impish spirit is the ghost of the island's first keeper, Major John Polereczky. Born in France and of Hungarian nobility, he fought for his native country during the American Revolution. After serving as town clerk in Dresden, Maine, for twenty-five years, he applied to be a keeper at Seguin in 1795. His paltry salary—$200 a year—was barely enough to sustain him, but it was never raised despite his constant requests. He served for about eight years before dying penniless on the island.

Another who is believed to have taken up eternal residence is a little girl, a keeper's daughter who died and is said to be buried on the island (yet no one knows exactly where). Her spirit has been seen running through the gardens around the lighthouse, laughing, smiling, and sometimes waving—a welcome change from the cliché of the dark and imposing morose ghost. Some have also heard her running up and down the stairs, cheerily laughing, or even bouncing a ball off the walls.

Meanwhile, other keepers have heard coughing when no one else was present (Polereczky was known to like his pipe, or perhaps it is the little girl, who likely died of an illness?), and doors swinging open and closed unexpectedly, and have described walking through chilling cold spots.

Then there was one particularly creepy instance when the light-house was being decommissioned in 1985.

Once all items were packed for shipment back to the mainland, the work crew opted to stay for the night before making the trek back. They ate and drank, conversed, then settled in, weary after a long day's work.

Then, suddenly, the warrant officer on the scene was brashly awoken.

Someone was violently shaking his bed and pleading, "Don't take the furniture. Please, leave my home alone!"

When he looked up, as he recalled to author William O. Thompson, he saw a man. But not just a man; he was strangely see-through and dressed in oilskins.

Yet the shaking soon stopped, and the officer just brushed it off as a tremor of the night, or maybe, as Ebenezer Scrooge of Charles Dickens's imagination contended, the result of "an undi-gested bit of beef, a blot of mustard, a crumb of cheese, a fragment of underdone potato."

However, the spirit wasn't content with leaving it at that.

The following morning, when the items from the keeper's house were loaded into a dory for the mainland, the sly ghost (or so it's said) continued to play games: The belongings were held in place by a chain as it was lowered down skids into the water. Then all of a sudden, the cable snapped and the boat and everything in it sank into the ocean.

Ultimately, the episode may serve as a reminder not to disturb the dead, who like us, follow their own time-worn habits and rituals.

Still unsure? Perhaps your fears or skepticism would be confirmed while serving as a summer lighthouse keeper.

The Friends of Seguin Island Light Station invite a couple to tend the light and stay at the "rustic" keeper's quarters every year from Memorial Day to Labor Day, although they warn that the island is "situated in the midst of some of the most treacherous waters on the Eastern seaboard."

Duties include greeting visitors and giving tours, maintaining the facilities and trails, raising and lowering the flag, managing the gift shop, and (much like the keepers of old), making entries in a daily log.

"The position is both physically and mentally demanding, yet forever rewarding and possibly life changing," according to the Bath-based nonprofit.

And maybe, even, the specter of the old captain, the axe-wielding keeper, or the little girl will present themselves; because they, ultimately, serve as the true keepers of Seguin.

Chapter Six

Pemaquid Point: Iconic Watcher

Life like smoke rising twisted into legend.
—John Updike

As you climb the thirty steps of the narrow spiral staircase, the light is muted, the endless tumult of the surf muffled. Then it's a hoist up seven rungs of a wooden ladder, a shimmy through a snug hole in the floor, and you're standing in a claustrophobic lantern room with barely enough space to outstretch one arm.

Around you is a 360-degree view of land and sea that have vied for domination for hundreds of thousands of years.

Forever seems visible on the horizon; the ocean stretches on and on, eventually blending with the clouds. Bumps of land in the distance are its only companions. Down below, waves run salty fingers over hundreds of feet of contoured rock, striated and stretched as if the sea has endlessly tugged on it in an attempt to claim it as its own. Beside you, the Fresnel lens is a work of art in itself, its ripples of glass creating optical illusions out of the sea and sky.

It's hard not to be absorbed by the loneliness that comes with the adamant wash of the waves and the whistling of the wind demanding to be let in through the windows. One could forget the whole world exists out here.

While all of the lighthouses in Maine are scenic and character-istic, Pemaquid Point in Bristol, for its part, is unmistakably striking.

The light was commissioned by John Quincy Adams and put into service in 1827, and it is the quintessential image of a New England lighthouse: white conical brick tower attached to a white Cape house, outbuildings including a bell house and an oil house spotting its flinty terrain.

Originally, it consisted of a thirty-foot tower, but it was later raised to its current height of thirty-eight feet. It was deemed neces-sary to keep pace with the area's burgeoning maritime and shipping trade—which, not surprisingly led to an increase in shipwrecks.

Today, it is not only one of the most-visited lighthouses in Maine, it was chosen to represent the state in 2003, its likeness appearing on the reverse side of the US quarter.

And as it has kept vigil on its stony outcropping for nearly two hundred years, it has been witness to the varied degrees of the human condition—love, happiness, heartbreak, tragedy—and has proven a haven for hosts and guests of both the earthly and unearthly variety.

LINGERING ON

The log book entry, dated to September 2008, starts out simple and casual, reporting a "perfect week" that was all bright sun and mild breezes.

But then the writer, identifying themselves as a fifty-year visitor to the Pemaquid area, adds almost nonchalantly that the stay at the keeper's quarters was "interesting," and that they had "only heard a ghost once at 3:10 a.m. slamming a door downstairs."

Pemaquid is unique in numerous respects, not the least of which is the fact that its keeper's house is rented out in the sum-mer—attracting many a curious landlubber, and setting the scene for spectral experiences of all kinds that are very often recorded in the historic building's voluminous log books.

One 2012 visitor, for example, described being startled by a loud bump and a slam at 11:00 p.m.—which were then followed, promptly and rather creepily, by the sound of a female voice singing indecipherably along to classical music.

"I have goosebumps on goosebumps!" the visitor recorded.

At Pemaquid to celebrate her forty-third wedding anniversary, the writer described every day at the station as an "increasing adventure."

Still, its ethereal quality wasn't about to spoil the experience, or even repel the couple. She ended her post by affirming, "We will be back."

Others, meanwhile, have seen a white-haired woman in a long dress clutching a red shawl: Damp and shivering, her apparition has been witnessed standing beside the fireplace, or walking the ragged peninsula. She does not acknowledge the presence of others—and she is flighty when approached—but there's no doubt that she is perpetually in distress.

Other strange events have included every light on all three floors of the keeper's house flashing on at once (and just as suddenly switching off); drastic, indiscernible drops and rises in temperature; and disembodied cries and screams emanating from the open ocean.

But what of the origin of these odd occurrences?

Some say they could be the resounding echoes of an attack by Dixie Bull, the pirate on the prosperous Pemaquid settlement in 1632 ("Pemaquid" is believed to be a native word for "situated far out"), or the nearby siege of Fort Charles by the French on English settlers in 1696. Then there were the numerous raids—scattered throughout the tumultuous history of the area's colonization—by Abenaki Indians, including during King Philip's War.

But many say its spiritual ripples reverberate to a tragic event in 1635.

On August 15 of that year, the *Angel Gabriel*, a 240-ton ship bound from Milford Haven with colonists and supplies, anchored in outer Pemaquid harbor. Many of the passengers disembarked onto the new land, but an unknown number remained aboard. The following morning, a storm that later became notorious as the "Great Colonial Hurricane" clamored in, bringing with it wild northeast winds that blew for hours, causing the tide in some places to rise twenty feet. The bellowing gale destroyed the prone ship, smashing it to bits and killing all on board.

One man who had de-boarded and was expecting to eventually bring his wife to the "new world" once he got settled, was so impacted by the catastrophe that he forbade his beloved to come. The two never saw one another again.

Two wrecks from 1903 could also have left spectral imprints. On September 17, the fishing boat the *George F. Edmunds*, captained by William Poole of Gloucester, and the small coasting schooner *Sadie and Lillie* were lost among the rocks off Pemaquid during the roar and bluster of a vigorous storm. Between the two, fifteen mariners died and only four were saved. "Nothing but splintered wood and twisted iron remained of the two vessels," the newsletter "The Lincoln County News" reported.

As a tragic denouement, Pemaquid Point resident William P. Sawyer, who interviewed the survivors and penned the event's history of record, was himself found dead near the lighthouse on September 17, 1945— the forty-second anniversary of the catastrophe.

Numerous other wrecks and drownings in the area could just as well account for the strong paranormal presence at Pemaquid; the sea can be unforgiving, her victims unforgetting.

ETERNAL CARETAKER

Today, though—in pleasant weather, at least—Pemaquid offers a calm and welcoming aura.

Visitors can browse its fisherman's museum, which is plentiful with history and artifacts such as decommissioned Fresnel lenses and a bilge pump from the *George E. Edmunds*, before climbing its filigree-accented, cast-iron staircase to a lantern room offering overwhelming views. Many also tread the paths of its flower-strewn grounds or explore its unique rock formations, which have been caressed smooth by the sea and are variegated with contrasting dark and light streaks (once aptly described as appearing as if they had been pulled "like taffy" by giants when they were still molten).

Listening to the hum of the tide while strolling along the rocks where kelp lays abandoned, tide pools offer hidden treasures, and seagulls hunker with a watchful eye for any errant bit of food, it's not a surprise to think that so many souls have chosen to remain here.

CHAPTER SEVEN

Hendricks Head: Souls Unknown

If the living are haunted by the dead, then the dead are haunted by their own mistakes.

—CHUCK PALAHNIUK

IT WAS THE EDGE OF TWILIGHT ON AN EARLY DECEMBER DAY: long after the leaves have descended the trees, but before the first snow has fallen—the world just beginning to settle into winter's dark desolation.

Normally, Charles L. Knight wouldn't venture out at this hour; as keeper of Hendricks Head sitting on the cusp of Boothbay Harbor, he had a light to tend to, a fire to keep stoked. But he had official mail that had to be delivered to the post office, a walk of about seven-tenths of a mile from his quarters.

He wasn't looking forward to the trek; it was nearly dark and the kind of cold that made you hunch into yourself. Most of all, it was completely desolate.

"There are very few houses near the post office," he recalled to author and fellow lighthouse tender Robert Thayer Sterling, "and it's a bleak place in the fall, after the summer folks are gone."

As he set out from his keeper's cottage, the scruff of his own footsteps on the dirt road to town seemed the only echoes in the night (minus, of course, the monotonous sound of the ocean that served as the background of his life). The empty houses were dark silhouettes against an ever-darkening sky.

"Never before had a night been so spooky to me as I wound my way over the long sea wall by the low beaches," he remembered. "I had an undefined sense of uneasiness."

Suddenly, very faintly, he began to hear another crunch of feet on gravel. He stopped. The sound was coming closer.

And then he saw something he wasn't at all expecting on this lonely road to town: a woman. She was wearing black and she was alone, walking with purpose. She seemed well-dressed and refined, with all the "'earmarks' of a woman of high degree."

He had never seen her before.

Being the town lighthouse keeper, he knew and was known by everyone. And this time of year was too late for visitors.

He thought to address her, another lonesome soul on this lonesome road. But something about her halted him.

"She seemed to be a lady of unusual dignity, who might take offense if spoken to by a stranger."

So he let her pass, disappearing into the night. He watched as she went, but, gnawed by the cold, he hastily continued on his own way.

Even so, he couldn't shake the thought of her. Why was she on that road at this hour? Where was she going? Where had she come from? Most of all, who was she?

He carried the weight of those thoughts with him into town and on his return trip to the warmth of his cottage, even as he lay down for the night.

The following morning, his fears were confirmed: News spread across town that a woman had gone missing. She had checked into the Fullerton Hotel the day before and had never returned.

Such an event was unusual for this small coastal town—especially once the visitors had departed with the birds—so its flustered and concerned residents quickly arranged a search party.

Blanketing the area, it didn't take them long to find her.

Or what was left of her.

Her lifeless body was found in the cove being tossed around carelessly by the sea. Once pulled in, she was discovered to be laden by a belt and a heavy flatiron, pocketbook still clutched in her hand.

The death was eventually ruled a suicide.

Years later, Knight lamented of the gruesome find: "Such an ending to a woman's life seemed to throw a pall over Hendricks Head, and over us who dwelled there, for a very long time."

And it seems, they weren't the only ones it cast a pall upon: The lonely, unnamed woman is said to linger in the very spot she chose to be her last.

It can be at twilight, during a full moon, or on foggy nights: the apparition of a woman, clad in black, sometimes wandering the shore, other times intently picking her way along the rocks, unaware or uncaring of who may be watching.

In some cases she is glimpsed as a mere flitting shadow, the kind that is very often dismissed as a flight of the imagination.

As Knight explained later, there was from then on a "dread" in passing along the road to the ocean that served as the woman's final earthly walk. Particularly at night, residents who had to travel down it were always casting nervous glances behind them.

And then there is the story of the mysterious black limousine that arrives on the anniversary of her death, pulling up near the area where her body washed ashore.

Of course, no one has ever identified or talked to the driver (or the passengers, if there are any), or written down the plates; the vehicle is as much of a ghost as the lady of dusk seems to be.

But who was she, really? A broken-hearted woman no longer willing to face the world? A widow (as her black dress would suggest)? A scout for rum-runners? (It was the midst of Prohibition, after all, and that could account for the limousine that seems to perpetually be on the lookout for her.)

The truth will undoubtedly remain a question mark; the mysterious lady forever holds her secrets.

SHE CAME FROM NOWHERE

Hendricks Head looks out on a bay of unknowns, the dark woman seen by Knight being one of its most enduring. Put into service in 1829 and located on the western side of Southport Island on Maine's Midcoast (an area now known as "Cozy Harbor"), it originally consisted of a rectangular stone house with a light tower on its pitched roof, appearing almost as a strange growth. It was later rebuilt as a forty-foot-tall standalone tower, unique in the fact that it is square (opposed to the classical cone shape).

Yet she is not the only restless spirit on this unique curvature of land. She has a rival, of sorts: Dressed all in white, a ghostly woman has been seen wandering aimlessly near shore, appearing disheveled and distraught, forever seeking out something she can never find. Her fate, it is said, came at the fury of a particularly tempestuous gale in March 1870.

In any case, both specters seem to be forever beckoned by the light.

As for the lady of dusk: To this day, no one knows for sure exactly who she was. All she left behind were fragments.

Ms. Meade, believed to be in her forties—but again, no one is certain—arrived on an afternoon bus in Boothbay Harbor on December 1, 1931. She was dressed all in black, carrying minimal luggage. Upon checking into the Fullerton Hotel (long since razed and replaced by a post office) under the name "Louise G. Meade," she began asking around the lobby where she might get a view of the ocean—the open sea, specifically, not the cove or wharves.

Her cover was that she was going west, and wanted to get one last good look at the ocean. The only other bit of personal information she offered was that she was a painter from Pittsburgh, Pennsylvania.

Pointed toward Hendricks Head, she began walking along Western Avenue to Southport.

Along the way, she passed Charlie Pinkham's General Store and the West Southport Post Office (both housed in the same building).

At the time, Pinkham's wife, Izetta, was working; but with bluster and cold descending along with the night, she crossed the street to her house to shut in her hens.

On her way back, she was startled to see a woman who she had never laid eyes on before but who she described as "medium height," and "not a beauty . . . but nice looking."

Upon glimpsing her, the woman stopped and addressed her distractedly, asking where she could get the best sweeping view of the open ocean.

Izetta, as had others in town, pointed her to Hendricks Head, but warned, "It might be dark before you get back. And it's lonesome."

The woman thanked her and continued, undeterred.

Not long after, she passed keeper Knight.

Upon his return, sensing something was amiss, he caught a movement: someone in silhouette behind the cottages. With it being almost too dark to see, he shouted out. There was no return response. He figured that, if there was someone out there in the night, they would see the lights of his house and the lighthouse, and seek refuge there.

But as history tells, the unknown lady never did.

Once she was declared missing the following morning, locals began scouring the shore, following the path she took on that fateful night.

At the shoreline, they discovered footprints moving in unsettled patterns; Knight deduced that they offered a key to her state of mind.

"It possibly might go to show that she wandered about before finally deciding to jump overboard," he said.

Back in her hotel room, her suitcase was found opened but barely touched. She had taken great effort to conceal her identity, cutting all the labels from her clothes. The only item she neglected was an overcoat from Lord & Taylor—now a luxury chain with dozens of locations around the country, but at the time a store exclusive to New York City.

Still, an official search party didn't set out until five days later, led by Charlie Pinkham, who was considered the town's "fourth selectman." (Although it depends on their size, New England towns typically have a board of three selectmen.)

Two groups swept the shoreline, one starting south, the other northwest.

Finally, they saw something in the water.

It was the strange woman; the undertow was bobbing her up and down like a piece of detritus left behind by a storm, washing her up "near the surface, then letting (her body) back into the depression about six feet under at that time of tide," Pinkham recalled later.

Knight, for his part, ran to the lighthouse to get a line and hook.

They dragged her body in. It was a sorrowful sight: A leather belt was fastened around her wrists, then run though the handles of an electric flatiron as well as her handbag. The fingers of one of her hands were hooked to her belt; the thumb of the other was tucked inside the catch of her partially opened purse.

Following the find, investigators came up from New York, but were unable to develop any leads. Exacerbating that, the woman's identity was never firmly established, and no one reported her, or anyone fitting her description, as missing.

"Wouldn't think a person could just drop from sight like that, would you?" Pinkham said later. "But she did. Nobody ever came forward to claim one thing about her."

So to this day, the lady of dusk remains an enigma. Yet she is not at all forgotten. Her unclaimed body lies under a giant tree in Union Cemetery in West Southport, identified only by an unmarked stone. Sympathetic locals, at times, have taken it upon themselves to flank her grave with flowers.

Even so, the kindness of strangers has not seemed to quell the troubled soul of the lady of dusk. Her apparition repeatedly walks the dark and quiet road to the lighthouse; perpetually troubled, her soul seems to be doomed to live out the night of her suicide, over and over again, for all eternity.

TREASURE WASHES ASHORE

The thunderous crack of a hull slicing open as it abruptly makes acquaintance with rocks and dry land; the vibration of a heavy impact; disturbed waves angrily reclaiming their space; screams; commotion, cries for help.

These sounds and sensations crossed roughly a half-mile of water and coastline to Hendricks Head keeper Jaruel Marr and his wife, Catherine, in the early spring of 1870.

Batted about by the ocean and wind, a vessel had smashed against a ledge just seaward of the lighthouse.

Fifteen-foot-high waves pinned the boat in place; as it began to break apart, its passengers and crew attempted to save themselves by climbing its rigging. But in the frigid temperatures, the torrents of pummeling water quickly froze—locking the doomed seamen in place, the rigging becoming a trap rather than a refuge.

Keeper Marr and his wife could only look on, terrified and heartbroken. To launch their own dory in the vicious storm would only mean their deaths, as well.

Frantic, with no other options, they lit a bonfire to let any survivors know that they were there and would come to help as soon as it was safe.

But the storm kept pummeling the boat and the spit of land, preventing rescue for hours on end.

Darkness began to enshroud the lighthouse; all hope seemed lost.

Then, the keeper glimpsed something bouncing in the salty waves. Rigging a safety line around his waist, he waded into the breakers, retrieving what turned out to be a small, bundled package.

Soaked and shivering, he returned to the edge of the bonfire.

As the heat from the flames warmed him, he inspected the carefully wrapped item in his hands. It consisted of two feather beds tied together but nearly soaked through.

Carefully, precisely, he cut it open. Inside was a box. Opening it, he was stupefied at its contents: a baby girl wrapped in a blanket—terrified, writhing and screaming.

Marr ran inside, where his wife, just as shocked and perplexed, took the infant, calming and feeding her.

And then the couple noticed something tucked inside the blankets wrapped around the baby: a locket, accompanied by a message from her mother that commended her kin to God.

Back outside, the storm raged on. Overnight, the ship was smashed into oblivion. When daylight finally reached its welcoming fingers over the horizon, Marr, his wife, and authorities discovered that there were no survivors; all, except the child, had been consumed by the sea.

This story is one of the most epic in Maine's lighthouse history; over the years it has inspired numerous children's books and novels, including Toni Buzzeo's *The Sea Chest*, and *Waterbaby* by Cris Mazza.

Although some doubt its very validity, calling it too reminiscent of the biblical story of Moses, descendants of the Marrs—many of whom went on to become lighthouse keepers themselves—firmly attest to its truth.

The baby was believed to be adopted by a doctor and his wife who spent their summers in Southport, and she was said to have quite the fitting name: Seaborne.

Yet maternal instincts are strong and impenetrable; long since the tragedy, there have been many reports of a ghostly woman in white frantically walking up and down the shore near the lighthouse.

Wherever her child ended up or whoever she became, her distressed mother forever seeks her out, determined to once again hold her baby in her arms.

Chapter Eight

Burnt Island: Ghosts of the Witching Hour

It's easier to dismiss ghosts in the daylight.
—Patricia Briggs

Suddenly, there was the sound of shuffling, staggered footsteps.

Crunch . . . drag . . .

Crunch . . . drag . . .

Crunch . . . drag . . .

As if someone had a limp or a bum leg.

It was around midnight; the young man was sitting at the kitchen table, still awake with his station duties.

He started at the noise—because it was a sudden intrusion, but also because it was a sound he knew all too well.

Could it really be the old man back to torment him?

Quickly, he tied a rope to the door. He coiled the other end of it fast around one hand; with the other, he aimed his gun.

When it seemed the footsteps were just at the entryway, he yanked the string and fired three shots.

There was no one there. Not only that, there was not a single sign that anyone had even been in the covered walkway.

Spooked, the young man stayed up until dawn's light crept its way into the sky, smoking cigarettes, thinking of old man Stockbridge and his cruel ways.

2:00 a.m. is the witching hour on Burnt Island.

It is then that the ghosts of this sentinel are said to make themselves known—irrespective of and unbidden by each other's presence, their deaths separated by more than three-quarters of a century.

Sometimes their gestures are subtle and fleeting: a shadow glimpsed out of the corner of one's eye, a door creaking open or closed, clacking footstep-like sounds from above or below—any of which the tired mind could attribute to the vanishing remnants of a dream, the imagination, or a case of the "alone-at-night willies."

But other times it is abrupt and impossible to attribute to anything (solely) inhabiting this earthly domain: ghostly figures pacing hallways or gaily dancing; items propelling themselves off shelves; loud banging and yelling that, when investigated, appear to have no obvious origin.

Standing guard at the western entrance to Boothbay Harbor, Burnt Island's light is built in the classically New England style (a tower of white brick), and much like its kin spanning the wide expanse of Maine's coast, it is not without its resident ghosts.

Located just off Southport and built in 1821, it is Maine's ninth lighthouse; the island it guards derived its slightly ominous name from the age-old practice of sheep farmers who regularly set the land ablaze to clear it and improve grazing conditions.

It sits perched at the highest point of the five-acre mound, surrounded by rocks and flanked by evergreens, and has the unique characteristics of a covered walkway connecting it to the keeper's house, a pyramidal bell tower, and even a helicopter pad.

And while visitors can't literally step back in time to an era when its ghosts held more earthly forms, they can have the illusion of doing so. During the summer, the nonprofit Keepers of Burnt Island Light offer a "living lighthouse" program during which interpreters portray the experience of Joseph Muise, his wife Annie, and their children, who lived on the island from 1936 to 1951.

All in all, it is a beloved locale for many. Writer Malcolm F. Willoughby described it as "one of the most beautiful harbor lighthouses on the entire Atlantic coast," offering a "tacit but cheery welcome to the waterborne visitor."

Ultimately, he said, "this lighthouse is a guide, not a warning."

Its spirit inhabitants, for their part, prove more of a menace.

AN ORNERY KEEPER STAYS ON

Benjamin Stockbridge was not known for his congenial nature: quite the opposite, in fact. He was ill-tempered, bossy, downright cruel when he wanted to be. Afflicted with a bum leg, he was keeper in the 1950s, living on the island along with his wife.

However, as he advanced in age and began slipping behind his duties, the Coast Guard felt it fit to send a young assistant to provide some additional vitality and muscle power.

It quickly proved a nightmare situation—in more ways than one—for the poor young tender, who relayed his story to author Greg Latimer. He was critiqued on and criticized for everything he did, from the way he chopped wood, to the length he trimmed the lantern wicks, to his methods for cleaning the glass panes in the lantern room.

Undoubtedly to his relief, however, he finally got a reprieve from the relentless abuse. Stockbridge, already being of ill health, grew even sicker and had to be shuttled to shore for hospital care.

The young man was left on the island in peace—if only briefly.

Not long after Stockbridge returned to the mainland, his young assistant was jolted awake one night at 2:00 a.m. The bedroom door flew open and a voice shouted: "The light is out! The light is out! You have a smoke-out!"

Jumping out of bed, the assistant found that was not the case. Eventually, he calmed down enough to go back to sleep.

The next morning, however, he received chilling news: Stockbridge had died in the night. The time? 2:00 a.m.

The young apprentice had the additional encounter with his old master in the covered walkway, but other than that, it seemed he was free of the crotchety old soul.

Others, however, have seen Stockbridge's gimpy ghost making the rounds around the island, up in the tower, or in the keeper's dwelling. Some tenders have even said the warning bell has been sounded by unseen hands at times when the light has temporarily gone out—the old man, perhaps, rebuking them for shirking their duties.

THE DANCING LADY

A seemingly carefree soul, she manifests herself in white bedclothes in the deep depths of the morning.

Seen by many a keeper, she is believed to be Martha McCobb, wife of James A. McCobb, who kept the light on the once-charred island from 1868 to 1880.

As was the sworn duty of keepers, the McCobbs kept a log describing weather conditions, daily life, and seaborne disasters. In one instance, on December 1, 1873, James described "very cold weather and much vapor flying," with passing vessels literally encased in ice. Meanwhile, on November 29, 1875, he reported the capsizing and drowning death of the captain of the *James Somes* out of Portland due to significant snow squalls out of the northwest.

Then came a personal lament: Martha's passing. It occurred at "about two o'clock" on March 22, 1877, James wrote, and was the result of "congestion of the lungs and cankers in the throat, stomach and bowels." Although only age fifty-three, she had been in "feeble health" all winter; yet according to her husband, she had still been able to be "about the house attending to her work until two weeks before her death."

James continued his duties without his beloved wife for three more years until 1880, and despite her passing, said he was never more "contended" in his life in his duty. "'Tis so much better than anything else I could do."

It seems that Martha maintained a similar affection for the station—although there are no known mentions of her specter by her widower, she has been said to make herself known to many others.

One night in the 1950s, for example, a lighthouse keeper's wife was awaiting her husband's return from the mainland; looking out the window, she was shocked and a little bemused to see a woman dressed in a nightgown dancing around a lilac bush in the front yard. Before she could react or address her, the whimsical danseuse abruptly disappeared.

The Kellys, keepers for the Coast Guard in the 1970s, had an equally bizarre encounter: They were jolted from sleep by the sound of loud creaks followed by a voice loudly calling their surname. Because it was the middle of the night and there was no one else around, they said later that they simply accepted it as the lighthouse ghost. When it had the occasion to happen again, they recalled, they hunkered down and pulled the covers over their heads until it ceased.

The late-night spirit got much more intimate with Henry Sieg. The last keeper before the light was automated in 1988, he reported waking up to see a woman in a white nightdress walking the hallway; he assumed it was his wife Joanne, perhaps unable to sleep, or checking on the couple's two children. Thinking he was alone in bed, he took the occasion to stretch out—and was startled to find that his wife was still lying beside him (and in a rather ran-kled mood, having temporarily been smothered in her sleep). Sieg jumped up to search the house, but there was no one to be found, and his children were fast asleep.

Meanwhile, other poltergeist-like anecdotes have included landline phones flying unbidden off their cradles, and clocks and watches that repeatedly insist on stopping at 2:00 a.m.

Still, given the gravity of the job, lighthouse keepers are not easily unnerved or dissuaded: Despite the late night intrusions, Sieg was disheartened to leave when his post became obsolete upon the light's automation.

"We're really losing something here," he told the *New York Times* News Service on September 18, 1988. "It's more than a home for us. It's a way of life."

With the tower automated now for more than three decades, we can only assume Burnt Island's otherworldly night owls con-tinue on with theirs.

CHAPTER NINE

Ram Island: Protective Spirit

I don't believe in ghosts, but they blindly believe in me.
—AMIT ABRAHAM

LIGHTNING RIPS THROUGH THE PITCH BLACK SKY, THREATENING
to tear it apart. The wind claws and pulls in all directions. The sea
is no less vicious: Tossing up wave after giant wave, it wrenches
the small boat about like a piece of cardboard, spraying its lone
passenger with water so frigid it feels as if he's being frozen from
the inside-out.

As he struggles to keep his craft afloat, the fisherman thinks
for sure this is it—he had tempted fate so many times out on these
dangerous waters, but now the sea was finally going to swallow
him up.

Another lightning bolt sears through the immeasurable dark.

And in that brief flicker, he sees a sight that chills him just as
much as the tumult of the wind and sea: a reef that is far too close—
and standing on it, a woman in a blaze of white, waving her arms
in a warding-off gesture. Remarkably, she does not seem to feel the
effects of the weather; rather, she appears to be insulated from it,
her white dress and fair hair are perfectly undisturbed, as if she were

merely walking in the park on a bright sunny day. It is only her arms that move, frantically pantomiming for him to get away.

With all his effort, he steers his boat in the other direction—narrowly avoiding crashing into the ledge at Ram Island. A seasoned sailor of Boothbay, he knew of its notoriously jagged rocks and onerous penchant for sending men to Davy Jones's locker; but blinded by the storm, he had had no idea he had been so perilously close.

The mysterious woman had saved him.

She is known as the "lady in white." No one can say her origin, or who she was or is—but she appears on Ram Island in the worst of weather to warn mariners away from the craggy spit of land.

She is part of a long tradition, both earthly and not, of sentinels guarding the seas around this island.

Today, a thirty-five-foot lighthouse tower stands just offshore of Ram's ledges. A substantial stone structure of granite and brick, it juts solitarily out of the sea, and is connected to the island via footbridge.

Getting it erected took decades of petitioning by locals, the delay due largely to the fact that it was located within just a few miles radius of more than a half-dozen other lights in the Boothbay area.

Built in 1883, its first keeper was Samuel John Cavanor, an old salt with a peg leg who would have made Captain Ahab proud.

Still, the lighthouse did not prevent all disaster; Cavanor continued to report regularly on wrecks, and the tower itself was not immune. Over its 130-year history, its walkway has been destroyed, rebuilt, removed and re-erected again, and the lighthouse lantern glass has been smashed and its fog whistle toppled. When the light was automated in the 1960s, it was subjected to both neglect and vandalism, and its antique Fresnel light was once even stolen (although it was later recovered).

The location of many shipwrecks and drownings since the days when men first took to boats, its name "Ram" seems fitting—but it was actually derived from the age-old farming practice of quarantining male sheep away from the mainland as a means to control breeding. (And although early settlers are known for their ruggedness and ingenuity, they are not necessarily renowned for their creativity in naming: There are a total of twenty-one Ram Islands dotting the Maine shore.)

Situated at the eastern end of Boothbay Harbor near the mouth of the Damariscotta River, the island is particularly perilous due to its low elevation and the snarling hungry rocks lurking just off its shoreline.

Locals and seafarers alike had long decried that it could easily be obscured in any kind of weather, from high seas to fog to rain and snow (in truth, anything but calm seas). It was so notorious that it earned the ominous nickname of the "dark old hole," and, as befitting of such places, all manner of witches and ghosts were sighted there long before the lady in white made her first appearance.

As a means to thwart disaster, locals at first took the matter of a lighthouse into their own hands. It started out simply enough: In the mid-1800s, when a fisherman nearly shattered his boat on the night-obscured island, he took it as his duty to travel out at dusk to tie a lantern down for his fellow mariners to see by.

Others soon came to share the charge, with the unspoken understanding that the first one in from the fishing grounds before sunset was to serve as the de facto lightkeeper.

Sometimes they left a lantern suspended in an anchored dory, or affixed at a high point on the island. One lobsterman even created his own makeshift lighthouse, enclosing a lantern in a box with windows on all four sides and weighted down with rocks.

Over time, however, the practice became spotty, then stopped altogether. It was then, as author and lighthouse keeper Robert Thayer Sterling described, that "the spirit world seemed to have taken a hand."

On a night of "stygian darkness"—that is, as dark as the River Styx of Greek mythology that separates the living world from the dead one—a sailor attempting to make it home to Boothbay reported suddenly seeing a woman standing on the shores of Ram Island, dressed all in white, waving a torch. She seemingly came out of nowhere, warding him away from the rocks just in time.

In another instance, a mariner was convinced he saw a ship consumed in flames on the edge of the island. He had become disoriented in a thick fog and was bound for a collision with shore just as he spotted it. Later, he returned to the island, but could find no evidence of a wrecked boat nor a fire.

"Not even a might of charred wood could be picked up," Thayer wrote, "and he was at a loss to know how the signal was issued."

Others have seen the lady in white standing stoically on the boat as it is imbued in flames.

In a few instances, she has manifested in sound; one seafaring resident unluckily caught up in two different storms recalled being alerted the first time by a loud ethereal pounding, and the second by the deep tone of a fog signal. In both cases, the dark was impenetrable, but he was able to turn from the sounds just as he barely made out the rocky outline of shore with squinted eyes.

It was later that he learned that there was no fog signal on the island—one would not be installed until 1897.

"He was positive that it came from the spirit world as a warning that he was approaching a dangerous reef," Thayer professed.

Still, no one knows of the willowy woman or her origins. Was she victim of a shipwreck bound by duty to warn others away from her fate? The widow of a sailor yearning to spare others her heartbreak? Or simply a good Samaritan ghost?

Today, with the lighthouse standing as a beacon at Ram Island, the occasion of her appearance is rare—but her legend, and those of her good deeds, live on.

CHAPTER TEN

Guarding Muscongus Bay: Franklin Island, Marshall Point, and Monhegan

If a story touches you it will stay with you, haunting the places in your mind that you rarely ever visit.

—NEIL GAIMAN

FRANKLIN ISLAND: A SOLITARY SOUL

IT STANDS IN SOLIDARITY ON A DASH OF ROCKS THAT APPEAR TO have been thrust up out of the ocean.

An army of trees stand clustered at a distance—almost as if, over time, they have cowered away from it.

Silent and dark, discolored and worn from the incessant gnawing of the elements, the forty-five-foot-tall brick tower retains a watchful, yet mournful air.

Long since shuttered, its outbuildings burnt down by the federal government, Franklin Island Light is, essentially, a ghost in its own right.

Maine's third-oldest lighthouse, it was built on its twelve-acre namesake island in 1807. Uninhabited by humans, Franklin is located just six miles off the coast of Friendship, a picturesque town with a quaintly welcoming name, and is central to St. George's River bay.

The area has the distinction of being a key maritime hub; yet also, conversely, it is considered one of the most dangerous locations on the Maine coast. That is largely "owing to the great number of dry and sunken ledges that swarm in every direction," according to a report penned in 1842 by the Lighthouse Board.

Not surprisingly, then, the island has been a silent witness to many a tragic shipwreck—so much so that it earned the apt nickname "Wreck Island." That moniker also underscored the need for a lighthouse on its shores.

Today, the loose craggy oval of land is a national wildlife refuge providing home to numerous protected birds—and perhaps, along with its lonely sentinel, more than a few ghosts.

One of the eeriest stories dates to December 1768, nearly forty years before the lighthouse was installed. It was then that the *Winnibec*, sailing from Boston, lost her bearing in a winter storm. She crashed to pieces on Franklin's dangerous ledges, her eleven passengers and crewmembers all drowning or succumbing to hypothermia.

Later, after the storm cleared, a group of fishermen from the mainland followed a waterlogged trail of debris to what ended up being the ship's final port.

Being the first to discover the tragedy, they were overcome by greed, taking the opportunity to loot the destroyed ship and disturb the stiffened, frozen bodies that were scattered along the shore. (In some versions of the story, even, they were said to have murdered off those survivors who barely clung to this world.)

Making several trips, they transported several kegs of alcohol, barrels of food, firearms, jewelry, and clothing back to their home port.

But it seems their avarice (as well as the cruel goddess of irony) got the best of them: On what was to be their final trip back with their score, a fateful gale blew in and stranded them on Franklin

Island. Using materials from the *Winnibec* to create makeshift shelter, they hunkered down for the night, still reveling in the luck of their chance find.

Not for long, however. It was said that, in the middle of the night, after gorging themselves on food and drink meant for the dead ship and her crew, they were awoken by intruders.

At first, they thought it was a rescue party—until they got a better look.

These were figures with gaunt, hollow eyes. Their pallor was a deathly blue; their clothes were bloodied and shredded; ice and crustaceans had formed on their exposed skin.

Enraged, the spirit invaders attacked the looting fishermen, choking them with fingers as icy as the depth of Hades.

The terrified mariners managed to escape—but not from the haunting memories of those frozen corpses returned to seek revenge.

Since, numerous rumors have circulated about Franklin Island. Some have described mysterious hazy lights floating around on otherwise clear, moonless nights; others have claimed to have seen the apparition of the split-open hull of an old schooner flanked by misty, glowing figures. There are even a few who have sworn that, when camping out on the island, they have been woken with a start, unable to breathe, the lingering feeling of death's cold grip around their necks.

Today, the island and its lighthouse remain both beautiful and mysterious; visitors (only allowed August through May when its menagerie of birds aren't nesting) get a breathtaking view of the bay as well as glimpses of sea and avian life.

They can also explore the remnants of the former light-keeping station, now merely mossed-up and grown-over foundation holes and torn-apart brick pillars. Deemed unnecessary, it was purposefully burnt down by the Coast Guard after it was de-staffed in the 1930s.

The tower is all that remains relatively intact, standing tightly bolted-up and surrounded by the architectural ruins of its outbuildings.

The inquiring mind can only wonder about the memories and secrets locked up in the tall brick structure as it keeps its lonely perch on the rocks, endlessly looking over the bay.

MARSHALL POINT: RUNNING ON EMPTY

It's said that he appears suddenly, and without a sound: Before you know it, a gruff-looking man brandishing a huge sword is giving chase, and all you can do is let the adrenaline kick in and get moving; because he's coming—fast.

But then, just as quickly, right when you feel you're about to run out of breath and he's set to slash you in half with his blade, he's gone, dissipated once more into nothingness.

This specter—running hell-bent and pell mell out of the darkness—makes its presence known along the road to Marshall Lighthouse in Port Clyde.

In a state with a coast literally defined by its lighthouses, Marshall Point, established in 1832, is especially distinctive: a classic white stone beacon connected to the mainland by a short walkway leading over ocean-tumbled rocks. Its striking image has even been immortalized in celluloid: In the 1994 film *Forrest Gump*, the namesake Vietnam veteran/shrimp boat captain/Ping-Pong champion main character jogs up to it during a life crisis–prompted run across the country.

But this lighthouse, serving as a chaperone to the eastern end of Muscongus Bay, also harbors a grisly past.

The story dates to the early 1900s, when the son of a local lobsterman was found brutally murdered.

Carl Bennett was the mariner's name; he was known for his penchant for drink and the terrible temper that accompanied it.

But nevertheless, he doted on his two sons. Ben, the youngest, was his favorite, and he spent many hours teaching him how to hunt and fish.

But that affection may not have extended to his wife, Cora—when Ben was twelve, she jumped off the town wharf and killed herself.

Ben, traumatized by the tragedy and suddenly without a mother to help wrangle in his young impulses, began acting out. Notably, he began hanging around with a tough crowd that prided itself on getting in fights, stealing, smoking, drinking, and prowling the streets after dark.

One particular night, the motley crew was making its way down the lighthouse road when, a little ways in the distance, they spotted a group of men unloading giant kegs from a dory onto the shore.

It was the midst of Prohibition, and the crew was strong, armed, and in no way interested in getting busted.

Somehow, they caught sight of the boys—betrayed by a simple rustle, a footfall, or perhaps even the lighted tips of their cigarettes—and quickly gave chase.

The alarmed boys ran back to town.

Ben, however, unfortunately fell behind.

He was soon captured by the men. In no mood for mercy, they dragged him to the edge of the road. As he screamed for help, they slit his neck, severed his head, and dumped his body in the adjacent swamp.

Then they fled, never to be apprehended.

But their brutal act seems to have at least retained some sort of spiritual imprint.

Not long after the killing, townspeople began sharing stories, hushed along sidewalks or hunkered over beers at taverns, about seeing a giant beast of a man, knife held aloft, chasing a blond boy down by the lighthouse.

In more terrifying instances, the gruff apparition has purportedly turned his fury on terrified locals.

One man, while walking with his wife and daughter down by the lighthouse several years after Ben's death, recalled that a figure enshrouded by the dark suddenly began following them. Once he got a good look, he saw that the pursuer was bearded, burly, and dressed in mariner's clothing, gripping a giant, sharp knife. As they walked faster, he followed suit; when they ran, he kept the pace.

Then, suddenly, hands on their knees as they inhaled and exhaled violently, out of breath, they turned around in horror to meet their fate—and their follower was gone. Only tall pine trees stood against the darkening sky behind them. It was then that they realized the man had made no sound. Not even his footfalls had echoed in the blackened night.

Meanwhile, in other cases, Ben himself has been spotted, standing in silhouette above the swamp where his young body was laid waste.

Perhaps he is waiting for eternity for the precise moment to exact his revenge—or maybe, even, he is seeking a long-awaited reunion with his dear departed mother.

Monhegan: Keeping a Watchful Eye
She is known simply as "The Watcher."

And, much like the 194-year-old Monhegan Island Lighthouse, she has kept a long and lonely sentinel.

Dressed in a flowing dark cloak that starkly contrasts with her pale hair and fair skin, she is seen walking near the lighthouse, watching the waves. No matter the weather, and no matter how she moves, it's said that her long hair and clothing never rustle—it's almost as if she is a living doll. Similarly, she leaves not even the shadow of a footprint on the sand or sea grass.

If and when she is ever addressed, she simply turns and says cryptically: "He WILL come again."

Pirate stories—including that of the legendary Edward Teach, or more commonly, "Blackbeard" himself—are sprinkled like salt throughout the history of seventeenth- and eighteenth-century New England. It's said that many a raider roamed the waters around the hundreds of islands off the Maine coast, stealing, pillaging, and stashing their goods where they could (ultimately prompting sleuths of all kinds to investigate their "lost" fortunes).

And there is evidence to suggest the Downeast area played a key role in ancient times, as well. Manana Island, not far from Monhegan, features unique runic scripts that have been dated to the year 1,000, and that some have linked to the Phoenicians or the Vikings (specifically, relatives of the legendary Norseman Eric the Red).

Monhegan, for its part, bears a long and rich history.

Located ten miles southwest of Port Clyde, its brine-smeared lighthouse was built in 1824 as a means to lessen shipwrecks in an insidious area that over the years has been identified on charts as "Washerwoman Ledge," "Pulpit Rock," or even "Dead Man's Cove."

All of this establishes the dark backdrop for "The Watcher": Claimed to be seen by many an old-timer, she is believed to be the young wife of a pirate who was left behind to guard hidden treasure.

When her husband returned, they were to be wed.

But he never did.

So, it's said, her mournful soul continues to roam the sands, forever on the lookout, forlorn but hesitant to relent.

Meanwhile, one particularly colorful story dates to Easter in the year 575, when an Irish monk named Brendan and a group of his followers landed on Monhegan in a reed boat. They soon discovered wild sheep, selecting one for their holiday meal, then located a safe dry ledge for roasting. But to their surprise, once they had a good fire going, the giant rock began to move—and they soon realized that it was not a ledge at all, but a giant beast of the deep, most likely a whale (which for reasons only known to them they named "Jasconius").

The island was used by the natives as a fishing station—"Monhegan" translating from the rather uncreative label "the island"—and European explorers relied on it as an important landfall because it is the closest bit of dry land navigationally to Europe in the northeast, and can be seen (in clear weather, at least) for dozens of miles out.

All told, its history is vast and bloody.

There are numerous stories of raids by natives on settlers who were either completely wiped out or forced to flee. One particular atrocity where it served as set piece for man's battle against himself was during the War of 1812.

It was during that erroneously named war (which actually lasted from 1812 to 1815) that the British vessel the HMS *Boxer* and the Yankee ship the USS *Enterprise* vied for domination in the Atlantic's tumultuous waters. The naval combat took place on September 5, 1813, captains Samuel Blyth of the *Boxer* and William Burrows of the *Enterprise* overseeing the day's bloody events.

As residents of all the surrounding bits of land looked on, the ships fired away, cannons creating consuming clouds of smoke.

In the end, the American ship was ultimately victorious—yet, tragically, both captains died, and in a morbidly poetic twist, they lay side by side in large box tombs in Portland's Eastern Cemetery.

And they live on in more ways than one, immortalized in a poem by Henry Wadsworth Longfellow:

"I remember the sea fight far away:
How it thundered o'er the tide;
And the dead captains, as they lay
In the graves o'erlooking the tranquil bay
Where they in battle died."

Maybe in death, the warring captains have at last found their reconciliation.

Chapter Eleven

Matinicus Rock Light: Enduring Spirit

It's a vast, devouring world, especially if you're alone.
—Clive Barker

Doors are replete with metaphors: They signify beginnings and endings; invitation and refusal; opportunity and lost chances; comfort and fear.

And very often, as is the case with a certain door on a desolate, barely hospitable island several miles off the Maine coast, they can reveal realms to the unknown.

Matinicus Rock is a thirty-two-acre sliver of granite located roughly twenty-five miles offshore from Rockland, rising out of the sea like a giant primordial beast. Remote, largely treeless and often gripped by a jealous fog that seems to want to keep it suffocated all to itself, the isle was chosen as a prime location for not one, but two, lighthouses in 1827. Constructed of wood (a decision that would quickly be regretted and later rectified), the twin sentinels were situated forty feet apart and connected by a stone building.

Just the simple act of getting back and forth from Matinicus proved treacherous; since it had a little cove but no harbor, boats made their landing by steering as quickly and as steadily as possible through the breakers while, at the other end, being hauled by help-ful hands so as to not be dragged back out by the sea.

Perhaps due to the rigors of life on the rock, the lack of readily available medical care, or simply Matinicus's sheer isolation, keep-ers didn't last long at their post. Many succumbed to illness or fell victim to tragedy. In just a decade, the lighthouse went through a succession of nearly a half-dozen tenders.

Gustav Kebbe wrote of the isle's inherent desolation in the *Century Magazine* in 1897; in particular, he relayed a quirky anecdote about a resident cow named Daisy. Mooing "pathetically," she could often be seen "standing on that mass of barren rock, the only liv-ing thing in view, the wind furrowing up her hide," he wrote. "She would gaze out at the waste of wild waters with a driven, lonely look, the pathos of which was almost human."

As a somber footnote, he added that the bovine had at one time found companionship in a rabbit, "with which she was accustomed to play at dusk; but the rabbit died."

As for the forlornness of the enclave's humans, it's said that one despondent keeper climbed up to the north tower on a moon-less night, strung a rope over the stair rail, and hanged himself. A bachelor living on the island alone, his death was not immediately noticed until mainlanders realized that the beacon had been unlit for some time. Still, although he may have escaped his earthly con-fines, it is said he never truly deserted his post.

After the station was rebuilt not once, but twice, the north light was permanently darkened in 1923—part of a sweeping, cost-saving reform by the government—and the tower was locked up. And that's how it remained for decades, holding fast to its secrets, until the Coast Guard took over control in the mid-1900s.

As they surveyed the property, servicemen unbolted the tower—an act that seemed to greatly offend the spirits it had so long kept at bay.

The door was literally and metaphorically opened to an onslaught of poltergeist activity. Its disturbed entities were said to flip furniture, fling open doors and cupboards, and break dishes.

Meanwhile, the beacon light, as well as others throughout the keeper's house, were said to turn on and off erratically, machinery constantly malfunctioned, and the fog horn stubbornly refused to blow.

Not surprisingly spooked, guardsmen ordered that the door once again be shut.

The activity immediately stopped, souls seemingly quelled.

However, whenever they had to return to fetch materials from the shuttered building, the strange occurrences were said to start right back up again.

So the tower remains a locked-up enigma.

A COURAGEOUS SOUL

Yet not all spirits are of the evasive, willowy, jolt-us-up-in-the-night variety. Some, rather, are as the ancient poet Homer envisioned— immortalized through their actions and heroism.

In that sense, young Abbie Burgess haunts Matinicus. An unexpected hero, she has become an enduring part of the island's mythos.

Fourteen-year-old Burgess moved with her father Samuel Burgess, invalid mother, three sisters, and brother to the wind-whipped isle in 1853, where it's said that, during storms, boulders are flung around by the sea as if mere pebbles.

Duties at the original station included constantly tending the whale oil in the lamps so it wouldn't congeal, as well as wiping reflectors clean of the thick soot that constantly coated them. Young Abbie was soon enlisted to assist in that work, along with her other responsibilities of keeping house and caring for her mother and younger siblings.

Her tenacious legend was solidified in January 1856. One day, her father departed the island to retrieve supplies from the mainland, leaving seventeen-year-old Abbie in charge.

"I can depend on you Abbie," he told her upon leaving, expecting to return later that day or the following morning.

However, a strong gale screamed in, preventing his return.

And not just for a day or two—he was forestalled for four weeks.

Abbie wrote of the relentless weather: "The sea is never still and when agitated it roars, shuts out every other sound, even drowning out our voices."

In its endless fury, the storm largely destroyed the keeper's quarters. Resolute in purpose, Abbie sought refuge for herself, her sisters, and mother in one of the towers, what she called the "only endurable place." She also waded through water so cold it felt like it was slicing open the skin to rescue all but one of the family's hapless hens.

And for the entire twenty-eight days, she persevered in keeping the light constantly burning.

"For some reason, I know not why, I had no misgivings and went on with my work as usual," she wrote. "Though at times greatly exhausted by my labors, not once did the lights fail."

There was a harrowing case of déjà vu, when, the following year, her father was again detained on the mainland due to storm weather. This time he was gone for three weeks' time.

Again, the fastidious young woman rose to the challenge, keeping the family safe and the lights blazing. And her father returned just soon enough; when passage was once again safe, he found his cold, weary family with just one egg and a cup of cornmeal among them.

Samuel Burgess was relieved of his post in 1860, but Abbie stayed on to provide guidance to the new keeper. His son, Isaac

Grant, came to the island with him; he and Abbie took a liking to each other, and were soon wed.

They became a light-tending couple, taking up a post at Whitehead Light Station in St. George in 1875. They went on to have four children (one of whom, Bessie, died as a toddler).

Abbie, for her part, departed the confines of this life in 1892 at age fifty-two, writing before her death of the love she had for the lights she had so carefully tended for nearly forty years.

"It has always seemed to me that the light was part of myself," she said, describing how she would watch it most of the night, unable to sleep and plagued by the what-ifs should it be snuffed out. "These old lamps on Matinicus Rock . . . I often dream of them. When I dream of them it always seems to me that I have been away a long while, and I am hurrying toward the Rock to light the lamps before sunset. . . ."

Burgess now rests at Spruce Head Cemetery in Rockland; in 1945, more than fifty years after her death, author and historian Edward Rowe Snow placed a miniature lighthouse on her grave in honor of her relentless resolve.

The heroine also lives on in numerous books (fiction and non-fiction alike), songs, historical reenactments, and the US Coast Guard even named a 175-foot buoy tender—located off the coast of Rockland—in her name.

Still, Abbie herself was more concerned with Matinicus's immortality.

"I wonder if the care of the lighthouse will follow my soul after it has left this worn-out body!" she remarked shortly before her death.

Some say that might be the very case; in addition to her abiding legend, some have claimed that the specter of a young woman can be seen standing by the keeper's house, waving to passing mariners, forever determined in her duty.

Chapter Twelve

Owls Head Light: Maine's Most Haunted?

A house is never still in darkness to those who listen intently; there is a whispering in distant chambers, an unearthly hand presses the snib of the window, the latch rises. Ghosts were created when the first man woke in the night.

—J. M. Barrie

FROM HIS PROSTRATE POSITION ON THE SLICK, ICE-CRUSTED rocks, the young deckhand squinted through the thrashing wind and the near-blinding flurry of sleet and snow.

If only he could reach the light off in the distance.

But it seemed so far. Farther than his aching, frozen, bloodied body could handle. And his spot here where he collapsed was welcoming in its own way. He could just . . .

No.

That was just hypothermia beginning to wrap its cold, deadly fingers around his wearied mind and body.

He forced himself back to his brutal reality.

He was colder than he had ever felt in his short life, his head was fuzzy, his body was becoming numb.

But he had to try.

Slowly, he raised himself up.

His hands were bloody from where he'd slashed and clawed himself out of the ice-crusted blanket before dragging his body over the side of the ship; as he took step after aching step, wobbly, hobbling, he left a trail of blood behind him that quickly congealed and froze in the arctic temperatures.

Almost there . . .

Almost there . . .

And suddenly he was bathed in warmth so shocking that it stung his skin and paralyzed his extremities.

He felt someone dragging him, conversing agitatedly, flinging questions that his cold-stunted brain couldn't comprehend.

But finally, although his tongue felt like steel wool in his mouth, he forced himself to utter a plea: The mate . . . his bride-to-be—they were still out there, locked in a frozen embrace.

ROCKLAND'S HAUNT

Mount fifty-three steep steps to a narrow, rock-studded base barely wide enough for the nimblest of climbers, turn around to behold the glistening bay below. An impossibly blue sky is mirrored in a quintessentially cobalt Atlantic; lobster boats and windjammers float calmly by the mounded humps of islands and the Camden hills; an American flag flutters in a breeze that, even on a pleasant day, threatens to steal the hats of the unsuspecting.

The stout lighthouse—thirty feet tall and featuring the time-honored motif of brick painted white offset with black trim and capped with an ebony-colored lantern room—stands as the protector of this hill. Circling it are paths beaten down by visitors and lighthouse keepers alike; hardy shrubs and menacing points of boulders as old as the ocean itself require careful footing.

It is a scene that, in 1891, prompted journalist Samuel Adams Drake to proclaim it "almost too beautiful to profane with speech when we are looking at it, impossible to find language to do it justice when memory would summon it before us again."

Yet standing on its promontory 100 feet above sea level, one can only imagine how forsaken and barren an outpost it could be when the sea and wind are disdainful in their relentless pounding and howling, and as brutally cold temperatures stiffen joints and harshly gnaw at any bit of exposed skin.

Owls Head is considered chilling in other ways, as well—some call it Maine's most haunted lighthouse.

Keepers and their families have lived with this juxtaposition at Owls Head since the tower was built in 1825, and several stories both eerie and bizarre have permeated both on and off its shores.

Located at the entrance to Rockland Harbor, the station is named for the outcropping on which it sits, which some say has been sculpted by time to distinctively resemble the visage of the wise, wide-eyed bird. Others say it is a bastardized English translation of its original native name "Medadacut."

The area was the setting for fierce fighting between natives and would-be European settlers—including one instance in which an English captain used the Indians' tactics on themselves, brutally scalping them.

Another time, in 1745, a ship was tricked ashore by natives; the captain's son, Thomas Sanders, was captured. His father sent a ransom of fifty pounds, but Thomas escaped, stealing his guard's gun and burying the ransom—which he eventually retrieved, but not until fifteen years later.

The light was deemed necessary in the early 1800s—and authorized by president John Quincy Adams—once locals began quarrying lime and a building boom commenced in the southern states.

It was this time, as trade and travel increased throughout Penobscot Bay, which served as the backdrop for one of the strangest stories involving Owls Head.

The Frozen Lovers

It was 1850, just a few days before Christmas. A remarkable storm suddenly whipped through without warning, sending five vessels aground.

One of them, a small coasting schooner meandering through the area, had been moored off Jameson's Point not far from the bay's lighthouse. Its captain had made the trek into nearby Rockland, leaving three aboard: first mate Richard B. Ingraham, sea man Roger Elliott, and Lydia Dyer, Ingraham's bride-to-be.

When Mother Nature, in her ferocity, hurled up whirlwinds of ice, snow, and waves, the ship's moorings buckled, then snapped. Despite the sailors' efforts, it was pounded and smashed about like a toy, eventually getting pinned against Owls Head's rocks.

As the storm continued to jostle and bat at the stranded vessel, it quickly filled with water, although it didn't sink. Instead, giant waves threw relentless spray across its bow, threatening to make a quick order of freezing its three trapped and terrified passengers to death.

Thinking quickly, the mate suggested they roll up in a blanket and lay together in the shelter of the stern, in the hopes that the icy water would provide a protective shell around the wool.

It did—but became a tomb instead.

Arctic spray still flying, the three bundled together under their covering, which quickly became encrusted with several inches of ice. The mate and his female companion soon succumbed to the cold, losing consciousness.

Believing that he was the only one alive, the deck mate contorted his body so that he could retrieve a small knife from his pocket; he then slashed at the frozen blanket with the blade. Once he could see an opening, he beat, clawed and ripped, bloodying his hands.

Finally freed, he crawled over the side of the boat and made his way to the lighthouse off in the distance; he limped, shuffled, and dragged himself across a narrow bridge of rock that was exposed by low tide.

Lighthouse keeper Henry Achorn was not surprisingly astonished at the man in his glaciated state. He quickly organized a rescue party of local men that rushed out to the wreck.

On the boat, they found the young lovers as they had been described, encased in ice, wrapped tightly in each other's arms.

They were presumed dead—but their rescuers didn't yet want to give up hope.

They laboriously dragged the frozen couple back to the lighthouse, where they worked away at their ice coffin with picks, chisels, and knives. They then laid them in cold baths, slowly raising the temperature by dumping in buckets of increasingly warmer water, massaged them, and stretched out their lifeless limbs.

Remarkably, the woman started showing signs of life; she was revived, weary, exhausted, and damaged as she was.

A little while later, her beau began to stir, opening his eyes and beckoning in slurred, halted speech, "What is all this? Where are we?"

They were rested, washed, and given water and bits of warm food.

Although it took several months, they both made a full recovery, and were married the following summer (and they went on to have four children).

The deck hand Elliott, meanwhile, never fully recouped, living with various ailments from the accident for the rest of his life. Perhaps understandably so, he didn't ever again return to sea.

But as he lived out the rest of his days on the waterfront not far from Owls Head, he never tired of regaling anyone who would listen with the story—and who could blame him?

(Forgive the pun, but) it was literally a case of love put on ice.

HAUNTING ARTIFACTS

A similarly odd story—but one that ultimately didn't end so well—involved the brig *Maine*, which departed on its first and last voyage in November 1844. Carrying a hull full of lime bound for New Orleans, it and its entire crew of nine completely disappeared after passing by Owls Head. It's said that keeper Penley Haines was the last to lay eyes on it as it sailed out of Rockland Harbor on the clear afternoon of November 9.

That is, until pieces of it turned up three years later. A passing boat dropped anchor in Rockland Harbor, carrying with it a mahogany chest, a ship's atlas, and navigation book that were all identified as belonging to the captain of the *Maine* and his mates.

When interrogated, the presiding mariner stammered ignorance about their origin, only offering the paltry breadcrumb of information that they were left behind by three Portuguese sailors who served on the boat for a time before jumping ship in Santa Cruz.

Could it be that the men had been involved in the *Maine*'s disappearance and feared capture? Or had the items just been "lucky" finds? Had the ship been dashed to pieces? Absconded by pirates? Lost in the rogue waves of the open sea?

The questions linger. Maybe someday the ghost of her ship will return to port to provide answers.

GENIAL GHOSTS

Meanwhile, the lighthouse itself is said to be rampant with paranormal activity. Several keepers and their family members have attested to strange, undeniable encounters—if more often than not of the benevolent kind.

One straggling soul has been nicknamed the "little lady." She has been heard in the kitchen rattling silverware and sometimes standing in silhouette in the windows of the keeper's house. In even more alarming instances, she has been glimpsed, in classic-horror-movie style, sitting in chairs in night-darkened rooms.

In the 1980s, the keepers the Germanns recalled a too-close-for-comfort brush with what they believed was her specter. One windy night, they told the *Bangor Daily News*, Andy Germann went out to secure items involved in the tower's reconstruction.

His wife, Denise, was surprised at his rapid return. When she addressed him, she received no reply, although she could see the indentation of a body in the bed next to her. Eventually, she asked whatever it was to leave—and it politely obliged.

"I'm positive it wasn't a dream," she told the newspaper.

The following morning, her husband told her that when he had gotten up out of bed, he had seen a strange cloud of smoke that briefly hovered, then passed right through him toward the bedroom.

But the "little lady" is said to have spectral company. The ghost of a former keeper, dressed in captain's clothing, has also made himself known around the property.

He is said to be of the frugal and diligent sort, turning thermostats down and polishing the brass of the tower's Fresnel lens (a pleasant find for human tenders).

At times, keepers have seen footprints in the snow that seem to begin from nowhere and track up the ten short steps and seven-rung ladder to the lantern room. His heavy footfalls have also been heard clomping up the staircase.

Claire Graham, daughter of keepers Gerard and Debbie Graham who served at the station from 1987 to 1988, for her part, was said to have had an imaginary friend that she described looking like an old sea captain. Once she was said to have burst into her parent's room using jargon common to an old sailor, telling them to keep an eye on the fog rolling in.

Yet not all ghosts are of the human persuasion. Another lingering soul is said to be a canine "assistant keeper" from the 1930s. Now buried close to the fog signal at Owls Head, Spot was a springer spaniel who "worked" with keeper Augustus R. Hamor. His duties: clutching the rope of the fog bell in his teeth, tugging it until hearing the horn blast reply of nearby ships, then running down to the water to howl until the boat faded from earshot.

Sometimes, during storms, his disembodied barking can be heard cascading over the waves.

Enduring Charm

Today, Owls Head retains its unique charisma atop its rocky perch. Visitors can view its lantern room, complete with one of the last working Fresnel lenses, as well as the keeper's house sitting on the hill just beneath it, which houses the headquarters of the American Lighthouse Foundation, a nonprofit preservation group.

Meanwhile, not far away in Rockland Harbor, one of its brethren keeps its own lookout; Rockland Breakwater Light is unique in both its style and its function. Unlike the classic cylindrical towers that dot Maine's shores, inlets, and islands, it sits on the water at the end of a stone embankment seven-eighths of a mile long. Also unlike other lighthouses, its construction took eighteen years, largely on account of the significant cost—$750,000—of hauling in and placing down 732,277 tons of enormous granite blocks.

The lighthouse, perched atop a two-story wood-and-brick building, was put into service in 1902, and was considered a "stag station"—that is, keepers didn't live there, but traveled out to it daily to ensure it remained lit.

Those making the trek to it cross its long straight expanse of boulders, which appear like the jagged teeth of a giant and could easily devour a leg. Kelp is strewn along the way at low tide, and the buoys of lobster traps bob with the dancing water and in the wake of passing boats.

The building itself seems a ghost, the paint of its exterior flecked off and mottled by the salty air, shuttered windows appearing like vacant eyes, some of their sills claimed by the elegant webs of diligent spiders.

Haunting both architecturally and scenically, visitors can only speculate the secret wonders it holds as it stands determined in its purpose.

All told, between those passing through and those staying on, earthly or non-earthly, there's no doubt that both Rockland lighthouses are a draw for enigmatic souls—in addition to being ones themselves.

CHAPTER THIRTEEN

Marking Mount Desert: Bass Harbor Head and Burnt Coat Harbor

Ghosts seem harder to please than we are; it is as though they haunt for haunting's sake—much as we relive, brood, and smoulder over our pasts.

—ELIZABETH BOWEN

THE ONLY LIGHTHOUSE SITUATED ON MOUNT DESERT ISLAND, BASS Harbor Head is a striking sight: It clings precipitously to a flat perch just at the edge of steep rocks that tumble sharply into the Atlantic.

For centuries, it has inspired many a poetic turn of phrase— Samuel Adams Drake described it as a "squat little lighthouse, in white cassock and black cap" sitting "demurely looking off to the sea," while Samuel de Champlain called its setting "ile des Monts Deserts" (or island of bare mountains) on account of its marked lack of vegetation. Others, meanwhile, have aptly likened the quaint structure to a dollhouse proudly posted upon its granite bluff.

For the thousands of visitors who descend on Acadia National Park each year, its classic silhouette has been immortalized in many a photo and painting, fringed by blushing sunsets, wispy clouds, or

101

tinged by the last bit of twilight, the flash of its unique red lens a striking highlight against the white of its tower and keeper's house.

But beauty, as the cliché goes, can be deceiving—this light harbors a lurid history.

The tragedies date back to the late 1850s, during its very construction. When the thirty-two-foot-tall cylindrical brick lighthouse was being erected in 1858, one of its crewmen suddenly went missing.

His concerned fellow workers were said to have discovered an ax, handle and blade caked with dried blood, hastily hidden away near the construction site.

But the man was never heard from or seen again.

Some would like to believe that he simply slipped away, tired of the aching labor on the rugged island with its barely passable roads and difficult mooring spots.

But others say his death was premeditated by another member of the construction crew—although no one could gather to guess why—and that, horribly, his body was disposed of inside the walls of the lighthouse.

In any case, the lighthouse has had a grisly history of claiming victims—or driving them away. Before the light was automated in the 1970s, many lighthouse keepers and their wives succumbed to various diseases such as typhoid fever, heart attacks or strokes, or suffered strange accidents. Not many keepers maintained their station there for more than a few years.

Coincidence? No one can say for sure.

Some, however, attribute the pattern of ill fortune to the ghost of the crewman entombed like Poe's Fortunato—they say he takes his vengeance out on the living by essentially trapping them in their own bodies.

But it's said he is not the only restive soul on this weather-beaten point. Others have reported seeing the silhouette of a woman in a rocking chair in a window of the keeper's house. Then there is the rumor of the old man who fancies sitting on a stump in the snow; sometimes he plays chimerical tricks and manifests as a deer—but he never leaves any tracks, whether animal or human, behind.

Close by, similarly mystical ghosts are also said to bend the boundaries between the known and the unknown realms.

Mount Desert has many distinctly beautiful, placid and pristine hills, valleys, and hideaways; among those is Fernald Point, near what is known as Flying Mountain, a popular hiking spot.

Beyond its natural charms, the area is a nationally recognized archaeological site. A dig in the 1970s revealed shell midden that date to around 1000 BCE—that is, mounds that are essentially ancient domestic waste dumps.

Hikers today are rewarded with sweeping views brought in on a salty breeze; little could one believe that this was once the site of a brutal and bloody massacre (and resultant spectral phenomena).

Fernald Point was the site of the first white settlement on the island, populated by Jesuit missionaries and named Saint Saviour Mission. The men were sent by a noblewoman named Marquise de Boucherville in an attempt to establish a French stronghold in the brave new untamed world (what the monarchy hoped would come to be known as New France).

But in 1613, the missionaries were murdered in a vicious surprise attack by a local fisherman who had been hired by the British to prevent French settlement. They came aboard the *Jonas*, attacking with sixty musketeers and fourteen guns, killing the majority of the settlers and capturing the rest (who at first fled, then, fearing starvation, gave themselves up).

Since, fishermen have seen white shapes flying around the area, sometimes accompanied by strange ethereal voices praying in French, or the rhythmic slapping of oars. Others have seen a man in brown holding a cross to his chest; but he is of the wary sort, fleeing as soon as he attracts attention. In other instances, boats rowed in by day visitors have simply disappeared—along with all of their other belongings—without a trace. While the common thievery of the living can't be discounted, the latter could perhaps be the act of the long-dead settlers looking for one last opportunity to flee.

Burnt Coat Light's Spiritual Trifecta

One is said to be a mourning mother forever clutching her child. Another is a lonely wife whose voice can be heard endlessly wailing for her lost husband. Then there are the young lovers who have spent eternity in exile.

Swan's Island is a tiny seaside hamlet located roughly six miles offshore from Mount Desert Island. Year-round, it is home to about 350 people—as well as, some say, a handful of local ghosts.

Once a Native American stronghold, the island was chartered by Champlain in 1604; it was later named for Colonel James Swan, an all-around Renaissance man who participated in the Boston Tea Party in 1773.

In 1872, Burnt Coat Harbor light was erected on Hockamock Head, an idyllic promontory jutting out into the bay. From there, lighthouse keepers and their families could watch the schooners shuttling by, and keep track of the changing temper of the sea.

Author Mary Bradford Crowninshield called the lighthouse the "snuggest and prettiest on the coast," and writer Robert Thayer Sterling described it as a "little place out of the wind and storm (where) sailors found restfulness."

But the area is said to harbor its share of the restless, as well.

For centuries, natives and settlers have described a frightening occurrence in which faces are illuminated by impossibly bright fires along the road to Hockamock Head (perhaps remnants of the local Abenaki tribe performing their ancient rituals—or something far older and more sinister?).

Meanwhile, Burnt Coat Harbor has earned the nickname "ghost hollow" due to its trio of ghosts.

One has been described as a woman in a flowing red dress; observed at low tide, she walks the mud flats mournfully, holding an indistinguishable bundle in her arms. Her footprints begin and end abruptly in the mud, then disappear to time altogether. She is thought to be the apparition of a young woman who suddenly disappeared early on into her pregnancy, her body later washing ashore.

She is accompanied in spirit by another young woman; yet only this lady's voice is heard, calling out to a man over and over that she hears something out on the water. As the legend goes, she and her newlywed husband were out in a rowboat for a picnic on one of the nearby islands when a storm came in; blind in the water, the couple was either drowned or unknowingly crushed by a passing boat. The warning words that cross the bay on the wind are thought to be the last the young bride may have uttered.

In an equally tragic tale—what you might compare to Maine's version of the age-old Romeo and Juliet motif—two teenage lovers whose parents tried to keep them apart disappeared one night and were eventually presumed dead.

Today, it's said, they can be seen on especially romantic nights—when the tide is low, the moon is up, and the air is still—walking hand-in-hand, never again to be separated.

CHAPTER FOURTEEN

Ghosts Way Downeast: Prospect Harbor Light and Mark Island Light

We leave something of ourselves behind when we leave a place, we stay there, even though we go away.

—PASCAL MERCIER

IMAGINE YOU ARE DOZING IN A ROCKING CHAIR ON A DARK AND quiet night.

All is still in the simple Cape house—an old soul, it seems to rest pleasantly along with its inhabitants.

Although there is the occasional punctuating gust of wind, the Atlantic has ceased its restlessness for the night. The wood stove pops contentedly; the ticking clock marks the early morning hours on the wall.

And then suddenly you have the very distinct, very palpable feeling that you're being watched.

There is a subtle scraping sound, barely audible, so much so that it seems it was the remnants of a dream, or perhaps the wind— maybe even an errant critter in the walls seeking solace for the night.

But it comes again, this time louder, more grating.

If not yet alarmed, you are intrigued, throwing on a light to check out your surroundings.

And then you see it. On a window marking the territory between the first and second floors, three small statues of captains stand constant guard, looking out over their mistress the sea.

Except, inexplicably, one of them has turned itself all the way around—and its empty, unblinking eyes stare right at you.

It might seem like a stunt straight out of *Poltergeist*, but statues that move seemingly of their own volition is just one of the send-icy-fingers-up-your-spine occurrences that have been reported at Prospect Harbor Light. Sitting on a sliver of land that, from above, appears as a finger raking the ocean, the lighthouse guards the eastern edge of its namesake harbor. It is located in an area known by locals as "way Downeast"—"Downeast" being an old nautical term guiding sailors to head "downward and to the east."

Built in 1850, the thirty-eight-foot-tall tower and its detached dwelling—a two-story Cape now known as "Gull Cottage," owned by the US Navy and available for rental by active and retired military families—is believed to be home to several mischievous ghosts.

One of those is said to be Captain Workman, father of John Workman, the property's last caretaker. Although the light was automated in 1934, John Workman stayed on for twenty years until 1954.

His daughter-in-law had only happy memories to share, calling it a "modern house" even though it didn't quite have the conveniences to match.

"The floors shined and the uncarpeted stairs were very handsome and beautiful as the shore and ocean outside," she recalled, adding that, "the outhouse with its Sears catalog and linoleum floor even welcomed you."

Apparently Captain Workman felt the same—a congenial man and copious pipe-smoker, he died in the cottage, and is said to have made it his perpetual home.

Many who have stayed at the property have reported hearing the unmistakable sound of footsteps, night after night, climbing up its stairs or entering the adjacent tower. Others have witnessed human-shaped shadows flitting across walls, seen lights turn on and off, or picked up the potent smell of pipe smoke when there have been no known smokers in the house.

In even eerier circumstances, visitors have seen the apparition of a sailor, enshrouded in smoke, rocking in a chair.

And there was the instance of one child, who, while being tucked in, looked right past his father and asked curiously but without fear: "Who are you?" His father, of course, was much more alarmed, especially seeing no one upon looking over his shoulder.

Then there are those pesky moving statues.

Lined up on a windowsill just above the stairs, the three figures are typically turned out to face the sea; they are three nautical men wearing coats, caps, and trousers and standing on blocks. However, the center one, a captain with a tie and a dark wool coat, seems to have a curious sensibility, turning around when he wishes to view the goings-on in the house.

Some reports, meanwhile, involve the playful presence of a young boy and girl. Believed to have drowned in the early 1900s, they keep to themselves without mischief, playing in perpetuity on the rocks just below the lighthouse, seemingly uninterested in the human inhabitants in their midst.

PLEASANT HARBOR?

Ghostly echoes reverberate in nearby Winter Harbor, as well.

The locale, across from Prospect Harbor by land and Bar Harbor by sea, earned its name from its unusual meteorological characteristic: No matter how cold it gets, ice never forms on its waters—thus ships can navigate it all winter long.

Its lighthouse sits on Mark Island, a rocky bump in the ocean just a mile from shore. Built in 1857, it was "retired" from service in 1933 and has been privately owned ever since.

It is from both there and the nearby mainland that, on nights of turbulent seas, locals and mariners can hear disembodied cries for help as well as frantic shouted commands of "Row, boys, row!"

These are believed to be the ghosts of the "Harbor Boys," a gang of Revolutionary Army deserters who targeted isolated villages up and down the Maine coast. Their tactic was to attack in the pitch black in unlit boats guided by oarsmen rather than sail, so as to go unheard and unseen. Once ashore, they terrorized towns by plundering and pillaging, raping women, setting fire to homes, boats, and businesses—and brawling with anyone who interfered.

Learning that they were in the area and not surprisingly alarmed by their terrorizing tactics, the townspeople of tiny Winter Harbor devised a plan: They would lure the attackers away from their village to the menacing rocks surrounding it.

Alerted by scout of the night of their approach, they extinguished all lights in town and placed lanterns on the serrated teeth of rocks that stood as guards at the entrance to their harbor.

Easily taking the bait, the harbor boys steered straight toward them—and then realized, at the last moment, as they saw solitary lanterns illuminating giant imposing boulders, that it had been a ruse.

Not graced with the quality of self-reflection—or, for that matter, the ability to recognize irony as it mocked them—they were said to have instinctively called for help from their would-be victims, their shocked helmsmen at the same time screaming "Row for your lives!"

But it was too late. Their boat was broken to bits upon the rocks.

And as some believe, they have been resigned to roam the dark, cold waters for eternity, reliving that night over and over much like the rock-pushing Sisyphus of Greek mythology.

Still, those who have lived at Winter Harbor's lighthouse—many of whom, coincidentally or not, have been of the writerly persuasion—have found both romanticism and sentimentality in its location and the so-called spirits that inhabit it and its surrounding waters.

In 1939, Bernice "Bunny" Richmond bought the lighthouse property for $2,000, and while living on the island with her husband, she penned two books. She and her family members reported hearing the sounds of strange visitors around the property on multiple occasions, but Richmond herself wrote of them without fear.

In one instance, for example, she described a "mixed group of people" who came down the walk, "chatting casually," feet scraping the cement. As they talked among themselves, they knocked "in a moderate way" on the door, yet didn't become discouraged when she wouldn't answer. Rather, they tried a few more times before continuing on.

"I don't know yet where my unreal callers came from," Richmond wrote, "or why they gave up knocking."

William C. Holden III, who owned the property in the 1990s and early 2000s, also recalled not-so-unwelcome spectral encounters: While lying in his second-floor bedroom at night, he could often hear discorporate voices chattering in the kitchen below.

To him, as well, they were not at all an intrusion—but rather, he considered them the true "owners" of the island.

"I became in my mind nothing more than a caretaker, entrusted with a gift," Holden wrote later.

A retired financial expert, he published a memoir in 2017 about his time on the island, during which he commissioned numerous repairs and even returned a light to the tower, which had been deprived of its light and stood bare and dark for several years.

Ultimately, no matter whose name is on the deed, the island and the lighthouse are not ours to own, Holden contends; rather, both "will forever belong" to keepers of long past, their families, fishermen who sailed the bay around them, locals, and "all who have been fortunate enough to walk the path from the boathouse to the keeper's house, through the field of daisies and foxglove," and experienced the magic of this snug harbor.

Richmond echoed those nostalgic feelings, recalling how "terribly important" it was for her to "sleep on the island with sea sounds encircling me," the morning bringing "that first rush of salty air through my kitchen door" and daily walks through "vein-like paths to the gardens."

Perhaps this is why so many have chosen to stay upon the sea enshrouded islet; it is a welcoming home, a haven for poets and hopeless romantics and watchers of the sea.

If ghosts do linger among us, it is pleasant to think that not all of them do so absently, or with malice or anger in their hearts.

CHAPTER FIFTEEN

Haunted Ships and Ship Graveyards

The sea is emotion incarnate. It loves, hates, and weeps. It defies all attempts to capture it with words and rejects all shackles. No matter what you say about it, there is always that which you can't.
—CHRISTOPHER PAOLINI

MAINE BEING WHAT IT IS, WITH NEARLY THIRTY-FIVE HUNDRED miles of coastline and dozens of craggy fingers clawing at the sea, it abounds with stories of haunted ships (and the numerous artifacts and remnants they have left behind). Literally hundreds of vessels that were tossed, dashed, smashed, or otherwise waylaid rest below the tumultuous waters of the state's shores—and sail on in legend.

THE (UNSEEN) HANDS THAT ROCK THE CRADLE

Elizabeth Skinner was a caring soul; she had four children of her own and couldn't bear the thought of one of them—or any child, for that matter—being hurt. This is why, when during a terrible winter storm (at an unspecified time not too long before our own) she heard a baby crying out on the water near her Machiasport home, she alerted her husband. He brushed off her concerns, preoccupied with many of his own.

But Elizabeth couldn't shake the feeling that something was wrong. She knew there had to be a ship in distress out on the waves; where else would the child's cries have come from?

The next morning she took a long walk along the beach, scanning the shoreline and water. To her surprise, she found a cradle in the sand; it was beautifully carved, and did not look at all as if it had been batted about in the salty waves. It was as if it had just been gently placed there by giant hands.

Not wanting it to go to waste, she took it home, cleaned it, and used it for her infant child.

But it wasn't long before odd things began to happen. During storms, the cradle would rock on its own—which she, at the urgings of her husband, convinced herself was due to the vibrations of the floorboards.

Then one day not long after, her sister came to visit. Although many laughed off the suggestion, she was said to have the gift of seeing beyond the realm of the living.

Upon walking into the youngest child's room, the sister was shocked to see a woman dressed in black standing over the sleeping infant. She was pale as death, and seaweed clung to her hair. The sister hurried to Elizabeth and asked who was that woman rocking the cradle?

Elizabeth, for her part, terrified and now fully convinced that the piece of furniture was cursed, had it chopped into pieces and burned. So the legend goes, as the cradle was consumed in flames, those present had to block their ears against shrill, unearthly screams—which stopped as soon as the wood was reduced to ashes.

It was a chilling lesson to Elizabeth that, although thriftiness can be a virtue, some things simply shouldn't be recycled.

Ghosts in the Mist

Suddenly they appear, many of them small children, water-logged, dressed in dark and heavy Victorian-era garb. Purposefully and steadily, they walk out of the mist near the Portland docks on or around November 27, the anniversary of their deaths.

It is said that they are the lost souls of the SS *Portland*, a side-wheeler that crashed off the city's rock-strewn shore in 1898.

It was the eve of Thanksgiving, and Hollis Blanchard, captain of the 280-foot-long Bath-built ship, was eager to return home for the holiday (as were his passengers).

In his haste, Blanchard ignored telegraphed reports about a strong blizzard approaching New England that was producing waves forty and fifty feet high.

The SS *Portland* almost made it; but not quite. As it was coming into home port, it was overtaken by the storm. All on board perished.

But its water-logged spirits continue to return—perhaps as an enduring reminder of men's folly? Only the restless ghosts know for certain.

ENDLESS CHASE

She materializes on still, calm evenings in Portland waters, fast in pursuit. With a sleek narrow hull and sometimes four, sometimes five, masts, she takes chase of a modern vessel, quickly closing the distance.

Participating in a race only her spirit mates are aware of, it is said she does not show up on radar, or leave any kind of wake.

When she finally does overtake her rival vessel, no crew can be observed on her deck, and her sails billow as if blown by Aeolus, despite a lack of any kind of wind.

The phantom ship is believed to be the *Red Jacket*, a Bath schooner that launched in 1854 and disappeared soon thereafter. She was particularly renowned for her speed, having once made a record-breaking cross of the Atlantic.

In both the earthly realm and the afterlife, she may have found a suitable equal in the *Whidaw*, a ship said to be captained by renowned pirate Samuel Bellamy. In the heyday of piracy as the new world was spottily being settled, he plundered all over the coast of Maine and southeast Canada, eventually creating a base in what is current-day Machiasport.

One day, however, his cockiness got the better of him. When he attacked a French warship in the waters off Nova Scotia, the *Whidaw* was damaged; when Bellamy then attempted to join forces with a whaling ship out of New Bedford, he was tricked to run his vessel straight into a sand bank, drowning him and all his crew.

Since then, the ghost of the *Whidaw* has been seen full-sail in waters all over the Downeast, flying a black flag, forever in pursuit of its next bounty.

WHERE SHIPS GO TO PERISH

It was as if they were floating tombstones.

Docked in shallow water, their naked wooden hulls were stripped of lacquer and paint and eaten through by the elements; their bottoms corroding in brine and mud; their masts mere skeletons long divested of their sails.

The phantom hulls of the *Luther Little* and the *Hesper* sat for more than a half-century along the Sheepscot River in Wiscasset, leaning against each other like T. S. Eliot's hollow men.

Everything reaches a final use—even, for all the money and effort that goes into them, seafaring vessels.

So where do ships go to die? Often they are dismantled, innards reused, the rest scrapped; other times they are dry-docked. In some cases, however, they have been anchored and left to the whims of nature, taunted by the fact that they remain floating in harbors, coves, rivers, or wharves, yet never shall sail them again.

With its bustling history of maritime trade, Maine has had a handful of such "ship graveyards"—including what came to be known as the "Wiscasset Schooners." Another location, preferred as the "Dead Fleet" or "Ghost Fleet," was Mill Cove in Boothbay Harbor; at one point in the 1930s there were nearly a dozen schooners left there to rot, some rafted together to save space.

For sixty-six years, meanwhile, the phantom hulks of the *Luther Little* and the *Hesper* sat just along the Route 1 bridge in Wiscasset—whose port, in its heyday, rivaled that of Boston—attracting photographers, artists, tourists, scavengers and those simply intrigued by the abandoned.

Yet few got to see them as they thrived in life.

Both four-masted schooners were built in Somerset, Massachusetts, around the time of the First World War. The 204-foot-long *Luther Little* was launched in December 1917, the 210-foot-long *Hesper* (whose name ancient history aficionados would recognize as a variation of the Greek Hesperus, the evening star) in July 1918. For much of their early lives, they were used to transport coal, oil, and fertilizer to ports all around the Atlantic.

Then, during the Great Depression, after being inert in Portland harbor for two years, they were purchased at auction by timber baron Frank Winter. Paying just $1,125 for both of them, he had them repaired and maintained with the intent of using them to transfer lumber cargoes to Boston and New York.

But Winter's operation eventually began to encounter problems too numerous to continue, and the once-majestic ships remained docked. For a time, a watchman lived aboard them; then in 1936 they were dragged closer to shore. There they remained until 1998, slowly ransacked of their usable parts, disintegrating into themselves as the water receded into muck, suffering the ravage of numerous fires.

When their remains were finally cleared away, they had deteriorated from majestic sailing ships into barely distinguishable rubble. Local craftsmen salvaged what they could and reused scrap for furniture and artwork, while some artifacts ended up at the Maine Maritime Museum and the Somerset Historical Society.

Today they live on in countless images, catalogued over the years as they decayed in plain sight.

They were, in a sense, tangible ghosts, the last fading remnants of a bygone era. And like many abandoned places, they inspired the imagination: What ghosts might they, themselves, have harbored, their long-lost crewmen fated to walk their perilously pitted decks, or cue up at their rotted riggings for a duty that was no more?

APPENDIX: AN UNRIVALED VISIT

IF YOU'VE NEVER BEEN TO A MAINE LIGHTHOUSE, YOU'RE MISSING out. If it's been a while, there's no better time to think about a return (especially now that you've been let in on some of the secrets behind their charm). While not all of the sentinels mentioned in this book are accessible to the public, and others located miles offshore take quite an effort and a cost to get to, they can all at least be viewed in some way or another in their entire splendor.

And don't just consider a summertime visit; lighthouses can be beckoningly beautiful in all of New England's glorious seasons.

You might even come away with a ghost story or two of your own.

SOUTHERN MAINE
Nubble Light, Cape Neddick
The lighthouse and the island are not accessible to the public, but visitors can take in its spectacular views from York's Sohier Park, which is open year-round. The Nubble Light gift shop is open from 9:00 a.m. to 4:00 p.m. from mid-April to mid-May, and from 9:00 a.m. to 7:00 p.m. from mid-May to late October. *nubblelight.org*

Boon Island Light
This remote isle is not accessible to the public, but it can be viewed in the distance off the shores of York. Visitors can also get up close via boat or aircraft.

PORTLAND AREA
Portland Head Light
The tower itself is not open to the public, but visitors can walk around it and take in sweeping views from all around its promontory as well as the connected Fort Williams Park. Its Cape Elizabeth grounds are open year-round from sun-up to sunset. A museum is open daily from 10:00 a.m. to 4:00 p.m. from Memorial Day to October 31, as well as on weekends in November. The admission fee for the museum is $2 for adults and $1 for children age six to eighteen. *portlandheadlight.com*

Cape Elizabeth, Two Lights
The western tower is privately owned and the eastern tower remains in service but is now automated. Neither is accessible to the public, but they can be seen and photographed from Two Lights State Park, which is open year-round from 9:00 a.m. to sunset. Park entrance fee is $5 for adult Maine residents, $7 for non-residents, and $2 for senior non-residents. *Maine.gov/twolights*

Ram Island Ledge Light
The light remains an active Coast Guard aid to navigation, but is not open to the public. Visitors are afforded nice views from Portland Head Light. The island can also be seen by boat.

Wood Island Lighthouse
The island and lighthouse are accessible only through tours offered by the Friends of Wood Island Lighthouse throughout July and August. Reservations are required and there is a suggested donation of $15 for adults and $8 for children. The lighthouse can also be viewed from a distance off the coast of Biddeford Pool, most notably from the East Point Audubon Sanctuary. *Woodislandlighthouse.org*

Midcoast
Seguin Island Light Station
The island is only accessible via charter/ferry or private boat. Camping is permitted by reservation from Memorial Day to Columbus Day, and there is a suggested minimum donation of $10 per person per night. Looking for a more up close and personal experience? Apply to be a lighthouse caretaker. *Seguinisland.org*

Ram Island Light
Not accessible to the public, but can be viewed by land from Boothbay Harbor, or via private charter or cruises run by the Maine Maritime Museum in nearby Bath. *mainemaritimemuseum.org/visit/cruises*

Burnt Island Lighthouse
Open to visitors from 10:00 a.m. to 5:00 p.m., and accessible by private boat or through Balmy Days II Cruises. The lighthouse and keeper's house are only open to tour groups or by appointment. A Living Lighthouse Tour is offered by the Keepers of Burnt Island Light from 2:00 to 4:00 p.m. on Mondays and Thursdays throughout July and August. *Keepersofburntislandlight.com;Balmydayscruises.com*

Hendricks Head Lighthouse
Not open to the public, but can easily be seen via boat, or from a public beach located not far from it in West Southport.

Franklin Island Light
Under the care of the Maine Coastal Islands National Wildlife Refuge, the island is accessible by private boat. The tower is locked up but visitors can walk around it and explore its remains. Please note: The island is closed to public access during bird nesting season, April 1 to July 31. *fws.gov/refuge/maine_coastal_islands*

Monhegan Island Light
The island is accessible only by boat, but is well worth the visit. The light tower itself is closed, but visitors can explore the grounds, and visit the museum located in the former keeper's house that is open from late June to September. *monheganwelcome .com; monheganmuseum.org*

Marshall Point Lighthouse
The lighthouse grounds are open daily, sunrise to sunset. The museum and gift shop are open from Memorial Day to Columbus Day; hours are from 10:00 a.m. to 5:00 p.m. on Saturdays and from 1:00 p.m. to 5:00 p.m. Sunday through Friday. *marshallpoint.org*

Pemaquid Point Lighthouse
Owned and managed by the town of Bristol, Pemaquid Point Lighthouse Park is open year-round. Its facilities, including the lighthouse, fishermen's museum, art gallery, and learning center are open daily from 10:30 a.m. to 5:00 p.m. from early May through the end of October. A $3 admission fee includes entry to the tower and the lantern room. *thefishermensmuseum.org; maine coastcottages.com/cottage/105*

Owls Head Light
Located in its namesake Owls Head Light State Park, which is open year-round from 9:00 a.m. to sunset. The lighthouse and the keeper's house museum are open from late spring to late fall, with tower tours offered by volunteers from the Friends of Rockland Harbor Lights. Check their website for a full schedule. *rocklandharborlights.org*

Rockland Breakwater Lighthouse
Spanning seven-eighths of a mile, the breakwater is open to the public year-round; however, visitors are cautioned during high tide

and inclement weather. The lighthouse itself is open for tours from 11:00 a.m. to 5:00 p.m. most Saturdays and Sundays throughout the summer; check the website of the Friends of Rockland Harbor Lights for full details. *rocklandharborlights.org*

Matinicus Rock Light
This one-time home of teenage heroine Abbie Burgess is managed by the Maine Coastal Islands National Wildlife Refuge. The grounds and tower are closed to the public, but visitors can view it (and its resident puffin population) via private boat or charter.

Downeast
Burnt Coat Harbor Light
Located on Swan's Island, which is offshore about six miles from Mt. Desert and accessible via Maine State Ferry Service. The lighthouse park is open daily from dawn to dusk. The keeper's house and light tower are both open in the summer months; check the website or Friends of the Swan's Island Lighthouse Facebook page for details. An upstairs apartment in the keeper's dwelling is also available for summer rental through Swan's Island Vacations. *Burntcoatharborlight.com; Swansislandvacations.com*

Bass Harbor Head Light
Located on Acadia National Park land and used as Coast Guard housing, only the lighthouse grounds are open to the public. Visitors are afforded a nice view via a vantage point off State Route 102A. *acadia.ws/bass-harbor-light.htm; acadiamagic.com/BassHarbor Light.html*

Winter Harbor Lighthouse
Now privately owned, the lighthouse can be viewed by boat, or by land from the Schoodic Peninsula in Acadia National Park.

Prospect Harbor Lighthouse

An active US Navy base, neither the light nor its grounds are open to the public. However, the lighthouse can be seen just outside the entrance to the naval station on Lighthouse Point Road, as well as from the nearby beach at low tide.

Sources

This book would not have been possible without the comprehensive work of so many authors, scholars, historians, and experts—as well as many a dutiful light-tender—who have tirelessly dedicated themselves to keeping light-houses literally and metaphorically lit for generations to come. I can only hope to do them justice.

Books

Bachelder, Peter Dow. *The Lighthouses and Lightships of Casco Bay*. The Provincial Press, 1995.

Caldwell, Bill. *Lighthouses of Maine*. Down East Books, 2002.

Cheek, Richard. *From Guiding Lights to Beacons for Business: The Many Lives of Maine's Lighthouses*. Historic New England, 2012.

Clifford, J. Candace, and Mary Louise Clifford. *Maine Lighthouses: Documentation of Their Past*. Cypress Communications, 2005.

Clifford, J. Candace, and Mary Louise Clifford. *Women Who Kept the Lights: An Illustrated History of Female Lighthouse Keepers*. Cypress Communications, 1993.

Gray, T. M. *Ghosts of Maine*. Schiffer Books, 2008.

Grenon, Ingrid. *Lost Maine Coastal Schooners: From Glory Days to Ghost Ships*. The History Press, 2010.

Jones, Ray. *Haunted Lighthouses: Phantom Keepers, Ghostly Shipwrecks, and Sinister Calls from the Deep*. Rowman and Littlefield, 2010.

Jones, Ray, and Bruce Roberts. *Northern Lighthouses: New Brunswick to the Jersey Shore*. The Globe Pequot Press, 1990.

Latimer, Greg. *Ghosts of the Boothbay Region*. Arcadia Publishing, 2015.

Latimer, Greg. *Haunted Damariscotta: Ghosts of the Twin Villages and Beyond*. Arcadia Publishing, 2014.

LiBrizzi, Marcus. *Ghosts of Acadia*. Down East Books, 2011.

LiBrizzi, Marcus. *Haunted Islands in the Gulf of Maine*. Down East Books, 2017.

Norman, Michael, and Beth Scott. *Historic Haunted America*. Tor Books, 2007.

Schulte, Carol Olivieri. *Ghosts on the Coast of Maine*. Down East Books, 1989.

Snow, Edward Rowe, *Great Storms and Famous Shipwrecks of the New England Coast*. The Yankee Publishing Company, 1943.

Snow, Edward Rowe. *The Lighthouses of New England*. Dodd, Mead and Company, 1945, 1973.

Stansfield, Charles A., Jr. *Haunted Maine: Ghosts and Strange Phenomena of the Pine Tree State*. Stackpole Books, 2007.

Sterling, Robert Thayer. *Lighthouses of the Maine Coast and the Men Who Kept Them*. The Stephen Daye Press, 1935.

Zwicker, Roxie J. *Haunted Portland: From Pirates to Ghost Brides*. The History Press, 2007.

Zwicker, Roxie J. *Haunted York County: Mystery and Lore from Maine's Oldest Towns*. The History Press, 2010.

Newspapers/Web-Based Articles

Baldwin, Letitia, "Life on Mark Island Lighthouse Inspires Memoir," *Ellsworth American*, September 27, 2017.

Belkin, Douglas, "Is Anyone There? Local Ghostbusters Investigate the Supernatural on a Lonely, Windswept Maine Isle, *Boston Globe*, October 23, 2005.

Bennett, Troy R., "This Ghost Ship Hunted U-boats in Portland Harbor . . . Maybe," *BDN Portland*, September 11, 2017, http://portland.bangordailynews.com/2017/09/11/history/this-ghost-ship-hunted-u-boats-in-portland-harbor-maybe/.

Dulce, Laura, "The Ghost of Goat Island Light," Seacoastonline, October 29, 2009, www.seacoastonline.com/article/20091029/ENTERTAIN/910290329.

Ellis, Annie, "Ghost Hunters Descend on Wood Island—Reporter Joins Crew for Night of Ghastly Investigation," *Biddeford Saco OOB Courier*, October 12, 2006.

Geiling, Natasha, "Maine's Most Interesting Lighthouses," Smithsonian.com, September 12, 2014, www.smithsonianmag.com/travel/maine-lighthouses-180951882.

About the Author

Taryn Plumb is a freelance writer based outside of Portland, Maine, whose subjects have ranged from ghosts and goblins to the intricacies of finance (which subject frightens you more?). She has always had a fascination with the paranormal. She is also the author of *Haunted Boston: Famous Phantoms, Sinister Sites, and Lingering Legends* (Globe Pequot, 2016).